The Bible Speaks Today

Series editors: Alec Motyer (OT)
John Stott (NT)
Derek Tidball (Bible Themes)

The Message of
Ezra and Haggai

To Thelma
Proverbs 31:10–11

The Message of Ezra and Haggai

Building for God

Robert Fyall

Senior Tutor in Ministry
Cornhill Training Course, Scotland

Inter-Varsity Press

InterVarsity Press
P.O. Box 1400, Downers Grove, IL 60515-1426
Internet: www.ivpress.com
E-mail: email@ivpress.com

InterVarsity Press® is the book-publishing division of InterVarsity Christian Fellowship/USA®, a movement of students and faculty active on campus at hundreds of universities, colleges and schools of nursing in the United States of America, and a member movement of the International Fellowship of Evangelical Students. For information about local and regional activities, write Public Relations Dept., InterVarsity Christian Fellowship/USA, 6400 Schroeder Rd., P.O. Box 7895, Madison, WI 53707-7895, or visit the IVCF website at <www.intervarsity.org>.

All Scripture quotations, unless otherwise indicated, are taken from the Holy Bible, New International Version®. NIV®. Copyright ©1973, 1978, 1984 by International Bible Society. Used by permission of Hodder and Stoughton Ltd. All rights reserved. "NIV" is a registered trademark of International Bible Society. UK trademark number 1448790. Distributed in North America by permission of Zondervan Publishing House.

ISBN 978-0-8308-2432-8

Printed in Canada ∞

 InterVarsity Press is committed to protecting the environment and to the responsible use of natural resources. As a member of Green Press Initiative we use recycled paper whenever possible. To learn more about the Green Press Initiative, visit <www.greenpressinitiative.org>.

Library of Congress Cataloging-in-Publication Data

Fyall, Robert S.
  The message of Ezra and Haggai: building for God / Robert Fyall.
     p. cm.
  Includes bibliographical references.
  ISBN 978-0-8308-2432-8 (pbk.: alk. paper)
  1. Bible. O.T. Ezra—Commentaries. 2. Bible. O.T.
Haggai—Commentaries. I. Title.
  BS1355.53.F93 2010
  222'.707—dc22
                                                                2010035595

P   18   17   16   15   14   13   12   11   10   9   8   7   6   5   4   3   2   1

Y   26   25   24   23   22   21   20   19   18   17   16   15   14   13   12   11

Contents

BST | The Bible Speaks Today

GENERAL PREFACE

THE BIBLE SPEAKS TODAY describes three series of expositions, based on the books of the Old and New Testaments, and on Bible themes that run through the whole of Scripture. Each series is characterized by a threefold ideal:

- to expound the biblical text with accuracy
- to relate it to contemporary life, and
- to be readable.

These books are, therefore, not 'commentaries', for the commentary seeks rather to elucidate the text than to apply it, and tends to be a work rather of reference than of literature. Nor, on the other hand, do they contain the kinds of 'sermons' that attempt to be contemporary and readable without taking Scripture seriously enough. The contributors to *The Bible Speaks Today* series are all united in their convictions that God still speaks through what he has spoken, and that nothing is more necessary for the life, health and growth of Christians than that they should hear what the Spirit is saying to them through his ancient – yet ever modern – Word.

ALEC MOTYER
JOHN STOTT
DEREK TIDBALL
Series editors

Author's preface

For many years now *The Bible Speaks Today* series, with its blend of careful exegesis and relevant exposition, has proved of immense help to Bible students and teachers and I was delighted to be asked to contribute the volume on Ezra and Haggai. At the same time I was somewhat daunted as although I have engaged with these books often, they seemed particularly difficult to bring to life for the contemporary reader. Ezra is probably less frequently preached on than Nehemiah, and all too often Haggai 1 is pressed into service to encourage a reluctant congregation to give to an ailing fabric fund. However, one of the delights of Bible study and teaching is that every part comes to life when the reader is genuinely open to the teaching of the Spirit. My former congregation in Durham used to smile wryly when I said of every new book we studied that no book could be more important. And in a real sense that is true because whatever book we are studying at a particular time becomes the voice of the Lord to us for that moment, and so it has been as I have explored and been blessed by Ezra and Haggai.

Both books have featured in my preaching ministry. In the early years I preached on Ezra in Bannockburn and first got to grips with its powerful message and its relevance to the contemporary church scene. In 2003 a series of sermons on the book formed one of my last series in my former congregation at Claypath (now Christchurch) in Durham, and I trust that it was helpful both to the many students as they passed through and to those who remained. Haggai I have preached on three times; most recently at the Scottish Ministry Assembly in 2005. A commentary always benefits from having been tested in the pulpit and although the final result differs considerably from these sermons, yet having preached on the books means that real people are always in mind.

The message of these books and their emphasis on building for God and the need of obedience to his word and openness to his Spirit is one which needs to be heard clearly today. The emphasis on the providence of God as he works behind the scenes and carries out his purpose even when little appears to be happening is an encouragement in dispiriting times. The pairing of Ezra and Haggai instead of the more usual Ezra and Nehemiah has enhanced my appreciation of both books.

This book has taken longer to write than it should have and I can only plead that two moves of home and job have often made writing difficult. I am very grateful to Ann Buchanan, formerly my PA at Rutherford House, Edinburgh, for typing the first part of this book, and to Ann McMahan, administrator for Cornhill Scotland, for a similar task on the second. I want to thank Philip Duce for his truly magnificent patience as successive deadlines have passed and further extensions have been granted. Alec Motyer has provided a continual and stimulating stream of comments in which mature wisdom and impeccable scholarship have been matched only by his inimitable humour. Often I have thought that his comments deserve publication in their own right as a wise and witty guide to the biblical landscape and I am deeply grateful. The bibliography shows the debt this exposition has to many others even where I have disagreed with them. However, one commentary in particular has been my constant companion, and that is the Tyndale Commentary by the late Derek Kidner. Like all his work it shows his elegant and concise style, his deep spiritual insight and his great learning which is worn lightly.

No book is ever written in a vacuum and the years since I was first invited to write this volume have been ones of great and sometimes painful change. During this time, as always, my wife Thelma has been a constant and loving support, encouraging me to continue with this project as with others at times when I was tempted to give up. This book is dedicated to her with my love and thanks.

It is a terrifying privilege to teach God's word, whether in spoken or written form, and I am painfully conscious of the inadequacies of this work. It is my prayer that the Lord will use it to bless others, not least those who preach and teach the Bible, and that it will honour his Name.

BOB FYALL
Glasgow
April 2010

Chief abbreviations

ANET   *Ancient Near Eastern Texts*, 3rd ed., ed. J. B. Pritchard
        (Princeton, 1969)
ESV   English Standard Version
JBL   *Journal of Biblical Literature*
KJV   King James Version
LXX   Septuagint
NIV   New International Version
WBC   Word Biblical Commentary

Select bibliography

Commentaries

Baldwin, J. G., *Haggai, Zechariah, Malachi*, Tyndale Old Testament Commentaries (Leicester: IVP, 1979).

Blenkinsopp, J., *Ezra–Nehemiah*, Old Testament Library (London: SCM, 1988).

Calvin, J., *Commentaries on the Twelve Minor Prophets*, vol. 4 (repr. Grand Rapids: Baker, 2005).

Cave, D., *Ezra/Nehemiah: Free to Build*, Crossway Bible Guides (Leicester: Crossway, 1993).

Clines, D. J. A., *Ezra, Nehemiah, Esther*, New Century Bible (Grand Rapids: Eerdmans, 1984).

Fensham, F. C., *The Books of Ezra and Nehemiah*, New International Commentary on the Old Testament (Grand Rapids: Eerdmans, 1982).

Keil, C. F. and Delitzsch, F., *Commentary on the Old Testament*, vol. 10 (repr. Peabody: Hendrickson, 2006).

Kidner, F. D., *Ezra and Nehemiah*, Tyndale Old Testament Commentaries (Leicester: IVP, 1979).

McConville, J. G., *Ezra, Nehemiah and Esther*, Daily Study Bible (Edinburgh: St Andrew Press, 1985).

Motyer, J. A., *Haggai*, in T. McComiskey (ed.), *The Minor Prophets*, vol. 3 (Grand Rapids: Baker, 1998).

Myers, J. M., *Ezra – Nehemiah*, Anchor Bible (Garden City: Doubleday, 1965).

Petersen, D. L., *Haggai and Zechariah 1–8: A Commentary*, Old Testament Library (Westminster: John Knox Press, 1995).

Redditt, P. L., *Haggai, Zechariah and Malachi*, New Century Bible (Grand Rapids: Eerdmans, 1995).

Sweeney, M. A., *The Twelve Prophets, vol 2. Micah, Nahum, Habakkuk, Zephaniah, Haggai, Zechariah, Malachi*, in David W.

Cotter (ed.), *Berit Olam: Studies in Hebrew Narrative and Poetry* (Collegeville: Liturgical Press 2000).

Thronveit, M. A., *Ezra – Nehemiah*, Interpretation Bible Commentaries (Westminster: John Knox Press, 1992).

Williamson, H. G. M., *Ezra, Nehemiah*, Word Biblical Commentary (Waco: Word, 1985).

Yamauchi, E. M., 'Ezra', in F. E. Gabelein (ed.) *The Expositor's Bible Commentary*, vol. 4 (Grand Rapids: Zondervan, 1988).

Other works

Ackroyd, P. R., *Israel under Babylon and Persia*, Clarendon Bible (Oxford: Oxford University Press, 1970).

Andersen, F. I., 'Who built the Second Temple?', *Australian Biblical Review* 6 (1958), pp. 3–35.

Bright, J., *A History of Israel* (Westminster: John Knox Press, ⁴2000).

Brueggemann, W., *Theology of the Old Testament: Testimony, Dispute, Advocacy* (Minneapolis: Fortress, 1997).

Dillard, R. B. and Longman III, T., *An Introduction to the Old Testament* (Leicester: Apollos, ²2007).

Ellison, H. E., *Men Spake from God: Studies in the Hebrew Prophets* (Exeter: Paternoster, 1958).

Evans, M. J., *Prophets of the Lord* (Exeter: Paternoster, 1982).

Kaiser, W. C. Jr, *The Messiah in the Old Testament* (Grand Rapids: Zondervan, 1995).

Kitchen, K. A. and Mitchell, T. C., 'Chronology of the Old Testament', in *New Bible Dictionary* (Leicester: IVP, ²1982).

Mason, R., 'The Prophets of the Restoration', in R. Coggins, A. Phillips and M. Knibb (eds.), *Israel's Prophetic Tradition* (Cambridge: Cambridge University Press, 1984).

Motyer, J. A., *Discovering the Old Testament* (Leicester: Crossway Books, 2006).

——, *Roots: Let the Old Testament Speak* (Fearn: Christian Focus Publications, 2009).

Robertson, O. P., *The Christ of the Prophets* (Phillipsburg: P & R Publishing Company, 2004).

VanGemeren, W. A., *Interpreting the Prophetic Word* (Grand Rapids: Zondervan, 1990).

Williamson, H. G. M., *Ezra and Nehemiah*, Old Testament Guides (Sheffield: JSOT Press, 1987).

Wright, J. S., *The Date of Ezra's Coming to Jerusalem* (London: Tyndale Press, 1947).

The Message of
Ezra

Introduction

Henry Ford famously said that 'History is more or less bunk'.[1] Many readers might be tempted to agree with him on first reading the book of Ezra. Not only does the history seem rather remote, an account of 'old, unhappy, far-off things',[2] but the events lack the strong narrative drive of say, 1 and 2 Samuel, and the forbidding lists of names do not help. Yet, as we shall see in the exposition proper, this is a superficial view and, if we make the initial effort, a rewarding and too often neglected part of biblical territory will show us startling vistas and reveal Ezra as a vital and stimulating book in its revelation of God's purposes and God's people. But we must first turn to the historical background.

1. When?

Ezra and Haggai must be understood against the background of the exile and the return. Both Kings and Chronicles end with God's people taken off to exile in Babylon. The northern kingdom fell to Assyria in 722 BC and the ten tribes were deported. However, Zion, 'the city of the Great King' (Ps. 48:2), remained; its rescue by the Lord from Sennacherib in 701 BC probably created a false sense of security in some, and as long as Jerusalem and Judah remained there was hope. This abruptly came to an end in 587 BC when the Babylonians under Nebuchadnezzar destroyed the city's defences, burned the temple and the royal palace, broke up and carried away the temple furnishings and devastated the surrounding countryside.[3] The mood is well expressed in Lamentations 1, where the city is a widow; a mourner and an object of mockery.[4] To use the title of one of C. S. Lewis' works, a 'pilgrim's regress' had happened: the

[1] Henry Ford, in *Chicago Tribune*, 25 May 1916.
[2] William Wordsworth, poem: 'The Solitary Reaper'.
[3] 2 Kgs 25:9–17; Jer. 32:43.
[4] Lam. 1:1, 2, 7.

people were back in the place which Abraham had left, and the land flowing with milk and honey given to them at the exodus was a pitiful, depopulated and desolate wasteland.

Hope was indeed there for those with eyes to see and ears to hear, and had been long before it happened. Isaiah had warned against triumphalism by prophesying the exile,[5] but then from chapter 40 he prophesies the return which was going to happen by the agency of the Persian king Cyrus,[6] which would be a new exodus.[7] Ezekiel, in his great vision of the valley of dry bones had spoken of how one day there would again be one nation and one King ruled over by 'my servant David'.[8] Daniel had kept his windows open towards Jerusalem and pointed to the end of history with the triumph of the Son of Man.[9]

The chronology of the return is as follows. The edict of Cyrus was issued in 538 BC and the first wave of exiles returned and began the slow process of rebuilding the temple, completing this in 516 BC, as described in Ezra 1 – 6. Then in 458, Ezra himself returned, sent by Artaxerxes (464–423 BC); this takes us from chapter 7 to the end of the book. However, that straightforward account has been challenged by many writers who argue for Nehemiah being followed by Ezra, rather than the traditional order. We shall return to that argument at the end of this section but meantime we need to reflect a bit more on the significance of the return from exile.

The atmosphere of the post-exile books seems bleak; the sky is grey and there is little sense of springtime and the freshness of new opportunities. But a little reflection shows the astounding nature of the return. To the onlooker the change from Babylon to Persia would appear to be simply the changing of one tyrant for another. No observer could have anticipated the policy of Cyrus of allowing captive peoples to return to their homeland. But while no-one could have anticipated this, the prophetic Scriptures, including the Isaiah passages already referred to, had anticipated just such a set of circumstances.

Yet the problem was that the glowing prophecies seemed to be unfulfilled. The desert was not blossoming like a rose, the nations were not coming to Zion, the throne of David was not re-established. It was a 'day of small things' (Zech. 4:10). It was, therefore, a day when faithful worship needed to be restored, faithful work undertaken and faithful living re-established for the day that would surely come when the sun of righteousness would arise with healing in his wings.[10]

---

[5] Isa. 39:5–7.
[6] Isa. 45:1.
[7] Isa. 51:9–11.
[8] Ezek. 37:15–22.
[9] Dan. 6:10; 7.
[10] Mal. 4:2.

The return was inevitably low key. We need only compare the possible three million involved in the exodus from Egypt[11] with the less than one hundred thousand who returned in the first stage. Moreover, the Abrahamic dimensions of the area between the Nile and the Euphrates had shrunk to a small province surrounding Jerusalem. To the north were the hostile Samaritans and to the south the inhospitable Negev and desert of Sinai.

The conditions in the land were far from appealing. The economy was basically agrarian and the weather could create havoc.[12] Moreover, the lack of infrastructure and leadership during the years of exile would have left a desolate land with deserted towns and villages. Morale was low and faith and vision hard to come by. Scripture tells us little of life in the depopulated land during the exile. Most of those deported were from the leading classes and the cities. Jeremiah 41:5 speaks of grain offerings and incense being brought to the house of the Lord during the exile, suggesting that in the desolate temple area some kind of limited worship carried on. The emphasis in Ezra is overwhelmingly on those who returned, their rebuilding of the temple and the renewed emphasis on the Torah.

A further significant piece of background (although not directly mentioned in Ezra and Haggai) is the importance of the community who remained in the land of exile, which is the subject of the book of Esther. The Persian king Xerxes 1 (486–464 BC) or, in Aramaic, Ahasuerus, is the king who dominates that book, although he is mentioned only in passing in Ezra 4:6. He is memorable for his unsuccessful campaign against Greece (perhaps the background to the feast in Esth. 1) in 480 and his defeats at Thermopylae and Salamis.

The chronology would look like this if we follow the conventional dating:

Dates of Persian kings	Dates of events in Jerusalem
539–530 Cyrus	538–536: First exiles return Temple building begins
530–522 Cambyses	
522–486 Darius I/Hystaspes	520–516: Temple building resumes and is completed
486–465 Xerxes/Ahasuerus	486: 'Accusation' of Ezra 4:6
465–424 Artaxerxes/Longimanus	468: Ezra sent to Jerusalem
	445: Nehemiah to Jerusalem

---

[11] Num. 1:46 records the count of males over twenty who could serve in the army; adding older men, women and children gives possibly three million.

[12] See Hag. 1:5–11.

I say 'conventional' dating because, as mentioned above, a strong body of opinion wants to reverse the traditional order of Ezra and Nehemiah and asserts that it was in fact Nehemiah who came first. Briefly, the advocates of this view draw attention to what they see as contradictions such as Nehemiah's apparent lack of knowledge of Ezra's proceedings over divorce; a thirteen-year gap between Ezra's arrival and his reported reading of the law and the apparent absence of much cooperation between the two reformers. Much of the argument depends on unproved and indeed unproveable hypotheses, and this volume (like its companion BST on *Nehemiah*) takes the view which flows naturally from the biblical material that Ezra did indeed arrive in Jerusalem in 458 BC and was followed by Nehemiah some thirteen years later. The reader interested in a fuller discussion is particularly referred to Kidner's lucid and magisterial treatment.[13]

2. What kind of book?

The overarching genre of Ezra is narrative. As such it fits into the grand narrative of the Bible from creation to new creation, and, along with Nehemiah and 1 and 2 Chronicles, more particularly into that recounting of Israel's history which especially from the post-exile perspective show us that God has not given up on his people or altered his purposes. As we shall see at various points in the exposition, the story of these dark days is linked with the story of the exodus and looks forward to the Messiah.[14] To explore this further we shall look at three matters: sources, structure and style.

a. Sources

Plainly a number of materials have been used in the composition of Ezra (and Nehemiah) and these are of essentially two kinds: personal reminiscences and archives. These personal reminiscences, often called the 'Ezra memoirs' appear mainly in chapters 7 – 10 and, some would add, Nehemiah 8. They add an unusual vividness to the book, especially since some of them are in the first person. We have an unusually clear insight into Ezra's character and motivation. Such phrases as *the hand of our God was on us* (8:31) and Ezra's own account of his dismay at hearing of the intermarriages (9:3–5) bring us close to the heart of the man. Further details such as *greatly*

[13] Kidner, Appendix V, pp. 146–158.
[14] See further the Introduction to Haggai, p. 141.

distressed by the occasion and because of the rain (10:9) add to the eyewitness flavour of the account. There is a sense of drama and involvement in the writing.

The other material plainly comes from archives. The decree of Cyrus (1:2–4); the various letters to and from the Persian kings in chapters 4 – 7; the inventory of temple vessels in 1:9–11 and the extended lists of names in 2:1–66 and 10:18–44 form the historical and factual context. By that I do not mean that the 'memoirs' are fiction but rather we are being shown both the public and private aspects of the return from exile. In the exposition the theological significance of these archival passages is discussed.

It cannot be conclusively proved that Ezra was the author of the whole book, although he speaks in the first person in chapters 7 – 10. Given the careful structure and unity of the book, the author was obviously someone of considerable skill and care. The picture given of Ezra in 7:1–6 suggests the kind of man who could easily have been responsible for the book as we have it. There is, therefore, no compelling reason to doubt the traditional attribution of the book to Ezra himself.

b. Structure

The book shows evidence of careful planning and of the highlighting of important themes. Some have drawn attention to the careful structure of Ezra and Nehemiah taken together.[15] The outline of the structure of Ezra which follows is the work of Dr Euan Dodds, one of my colleagues at St. George's Tron, Glasgow.[16]

First Return (chs. 1 – 6)		Second Return (chs. 7 – 10)	
1:1–11	Imperial decree Return of pioneers	7:1–28	Imperial decree Return of Ezra
2:1–70	List of returned exiles	8:1–14	List of returned exiles
3:1–13	Preparation and feast Role of the Levites Completion and ceremony	8:15–36	Preparation and fast Role of the Levites Completion and ceremony

[15] See especially the painstaking work of D. D. Dorsey in *The Literary Structure of the Old Testament: A Commentary on Genesis – Malachi* (Grand Rapids: Baker, 1999), pp. 158–161.

[16] I have altered a few details and added some comments, but the structure is the work of Dr Dodds and I am very grateful to him.

First Return (chs. 1 – 6)		Second Return (chs. 7 – 10)
First challenge		*Second challenge*
4:1–24 Pagans want to join Israel	9:1–5	Israel joins pagans
External opposition		Internal conflict
Petition to king		Petition to God
Resolution		*Resolution*
5 – 6 Prophets Haggai and	9 – 10	Ezra the priest
Zechariah challenge		challenges the people
the people		
The proclamation of Cyrus		Proclamation of Ezra
Purity of priests and		
Levites		Purity of people
Passover		

A number of points emerge from this structure. Plainly the two parts of the book have been constructed to bring out that these two sets of events some eighty years apart are closely parallel, with similar discouragements, opportunities, temptations and remedies. One is the work of pioneers, the other of a consolidator; both similarities and differences are noted in the body of the exposition.

In both parts (2:1–70 and 8:1–14) the lists of individual names show that this was an enterprise involving individuals and not simply a kind of mass migration.

Both parts have the same pattern of early progress marked by a ceremony of rejoicing and both show opposition to the work, albeit of different kinds. Moreover, the impetus in both parts is the Torah. The exposition draws attention to the echoes of Moses and other Scriptures, in the first part the work of Haggai and Zechariah and in the second the work of Ezra himself. But the undergirding of both parts is the reinstating of the authoritative words of Moses as the foundation of the new community's life.

c. Style

The book, as already noted, is a combination of narrative, archival material and personal memoir. This blend of material allows the reader to see this great event of the return to the land from a number of perspectives. The archival parts, while not especially interesting to the reader, are a glimpse of the actual people who took part in the return and of its human realities.

The narrative parts not only place the events in the context of world history, especially the Persian Empire, but also link with the wider biblical narrative. The exposition will explore many of these links, especially with Moses and the exodus. Both archival and narrative parts look to the wider picture and to its underlying meaning and the result is a satisfying blend of the public and the personal.

3. Leading themes

Considerations of history and sources are not in themselves particularly significant except insofar as they contribute to our understanding of the theological message of the book and its application for our own times. In particular Ezra presents four main themes: God; the worship of God; the people of God; Scripture and prayer.

a. God

We understand the Bible best when we begin with what God says and what is said about him. The presentation of God in Ezra, of course, is in the mainstream of biblical revelation. He is the God of Genesis 1, awesome and sovereign, who creates by his word and commands by that word all that he creates. He is the God of Genesis 2, close to, indeed coming down into, creation and having fellowship with the humans he has made. In Ezra this first aspect of God is most clearly seen in such phrases as *God of heaven* (1:2; 5:11; 6:9), which show God's sovereignty over both creation and the sweep of history. The second aspect is shown in the way in which the Lord *moved the heart of Cyrus* (1:1), and a similar comment on Artaxerxes (7:27) as well as the references to the *gracious hand of our God* (8:22, 31).

Intertwined with this is the emphasis on the faithfulness of God to his covenant. This is especially crystallized in 3:10–11 when the foundations of the temple are laid and the priests and Levites burst into a song of praise to the Lord: *He is good; his love to Israel endures for ever.* However, the theme is central to the whole book, with its emphasis on the continuity of the returned exiles with the earlier and more extensive community whom God had long before brought into the promised land.

Such a God could never be an indifferent spectator and the simple but heartfelt phrase *he answered our prayer* (8:23) shows the consciousness of divine protection though the whole enterprise and the sense of his overruling providence in both great and small matters. This was not, however, a cause for complacency, because another emphasis, especially in chapters 9 and 10 is God's awesome holiness. When the exiles returned from Babylon and rebuilt the temple they did not set up Asherah poles or worship on the High Places. However, they sat lightly to the Torah and repeated the intermarrying with foreign women which had led their ancestors away from the Lord in the first place. The concern for this is given expression in Ezra's great prayer (9:5–15) and underlines that the greatest need of the people was not physical release from exile but forgiveness from sin and a changed heart.

Nothing can be more important for the church today than to recover that sense of the greatness and graciousness of God and to have a renewed vision of his holiness. In such a renewed understanding of God and a deeper sense of his presence lies the key to progress and usefulness. A prayerful and reverent study of Ezra would greatly contribute to such a desirable outcome.

b. The worship of God

This includes first the regular worship of God of which the temple was the necessary focus. This is why the first action of the returned exiles is to *build the altar of the God of Israel to sacrifice burnt offerings on it, in accordance with what is written in the Law of Moses the man of God* (3:2). Before anything else, offerings needed to be made for the sin of the people to keep open the way into the holy place. The following verses further speak of the reinstitution of the other regular offerings and the preparing for the rebuilding of the temple. The rhythms of regular worship, disrupted by the exile, needed to be restored.[17] The culmination of the public worship of God comes in chapter 6 with the dedication of the temple and the celebration of the Passover. The reference to the *Book of Moses* (6:18) shows that the sacrificial system and the other provisions of the Torah were already well known before Ezra came.

At the heart of the worship of God in the book of Ezra is the emphasis on prayer. This is particularly embodied in Ezra's prayer in chapter 9. Here Ezra shows true leadership in that, although he is not personally guilty, he shares the sin of this people. However, this prayer is no morbid introspection because it leads to drastic action. Ezra was no mere pragmatist; his activities were rooted in listening to God and obeying his words. Neither was he a dreamer; with him faith and works were not divorced.

c. The people of God

In many ways the situation of God's people was rather dispiriting. Some 50,000 returned from exile;[18] this was *a remnant that has*

---

[17] See the exposition of ch. 3 for a further discussion on the theme of the worship of God and its relationship to the whole of life.
[18] 2:64–65.

escaped (9:15, ESV). Yet in this lay possibilities of renewal. The first emphasis is on continuity with historic Israel before the exile. Thus in chapter 2, although the return is to Jerusalem and Judah, those who returned are called *the men of the people of Israel* (2:2) and 2:59 speaks of the need to *show that their families were descended from Israel.* This is reinforced by the emphasis on obeying *the Law of Moses the man of God* (3:2; cf. 7:10; 10:3). This small community was organically related to the people of God who left Egypt and were constituted as such at Sinai.

The other aspect of continuity is separation from paganism. The *holy race* (9:2) had to be preserved. The nations mentioned here[19] deliberately echo earlier warnings about the danger of contamination.[20] This was balanced by a gracious acceptance of those *who had separated themselves from the unclean practices of their Gentile neighbours in order to seek the* LORD, *the God of Israel* (6:21).

The exile had put an end to Judah's status as an independent nation. Thus the concern to identify the returned exiles not only with the kingdom of Judah, but with the undivided monarchy and the people who gathered at Sinai to hear the word of God is a prominent feature of Ezra (and of Nehemiah and Chronicles). This was mainly to be achieved by worship (hence the crucial importance of the temple) and by becoming the people of the Torah. This renewed concern, exemplified in and encouraged by Ezra himself, is both a return to roots and a charter for the future.

Much of what we find here is particularly relevant for the long-established churches of the western world which so often fail to be a prophetic voice but instead produce a weak echo of fashionable opinions. The need for a renewed commitment to the Bible and a passion for its study, exposition and application remains the paramount need for the health of the people of God. The portrait of Ezra himself in 7:10, along with that other portrait of the preacher/teacher in Ecclesiastes 12:9–10 remains an inspiration and challenge to all who teach the word of God, not only in large gatherings but to small groups and individuals. The principles laid down, of diligent study, careful obedience and thorough teaching, are relevant to every generation.

d. Scripture

As will be pointed out in the exposition, Scripture is integral to the way the story is told, with references to Jeremiah, the Psalms and

---

[19] See the exposition of ch. 9.
[20] See e.g. Gen. 15:19–21; Exod. 3:8, 17; 13:5; 34:11.

other parts of the canon, as well as the fundamental importance of Torah. Ezra's teaching of the Torah[21] was a response to the situation envisaged in Malachi where the priests are castigated for their failure to teach.[22] Kidner[23] compares the situation to the power unleashed by the rediscovery and renewed teaching of the Bible at the Reformation, and such has always been the effect when biblical expository ministry has been reintroduced to a church which has grown cold and careless. Giving Scripture to the people is an urgent and never-ending task.

That it is not merely a question of detailed study of a book, however foundational that may be, is shown in various ways. Ezra 9:4 speaks of *everyone who trembled at the words of the God of Israel*, and such an attitude is a world away from mere law-keeping and observing regulations. This does not mean that detailed obedience was not necessary, and 3:2 notes that the altar was built and sacrifices offered on it *in accordance with what is written in the Law of Moses the man of God*.

4. Continuing relevance

The above comments and others throughout the exposition demonstrate the continuing relevance and importance of Ezra and I want now to draw some threads together. Three things can be said.

a. God never abandons his purpose

Granted that this return from exile was low key and the glowing promises of, for example, Isaiah 2 and Micah 4 of the nations streaming to Zion and the end of sin and violence had not happened, yet this was an important partial fulfilment which was a guarantee that one day that purpose would be reality. Such conviction sustains God's people in days of deadness and gives hope and expectation when there is little to encourage.

b. God never gives up on his people

The exile, on the face of it, looked as if he had abandoned the covenant people and washed his hands of them. Yet the emphasis of Ezra (as the exposition points out) is that the return is a new exodus. Pagan monarchs, hostile officials and discouragement notwithstanding, God's people have at least partially returned to Zion and have

---

[21] See exposition of ch. 7.
[22] Mal. 2:6–9.
[23] Kidner, p. 26.

resumed worship and Torah observance, which not only looks back to the youth of the nation but forward to the final gathering of God's people in the new Jerusalem.

c. God gives light for the guidance of his people

The emphasis on Scripture is the same as that in 2 Peter 1:19 where the word of the prophets is described as 'a light shining in a dark place, until the day dawns and the morning star rises in your hearts'. Ezra itself is part of that Scripture which helps us to walk safely through the darkness of this world until the day when all the promises are fulfilled and the dwelling of God is with humans.

Ezra 1:1–11
1. The ransomed of the Lord return

Visiting a show house is always an enjoyable experience and the smell of new wood, gleaming surfaces and fresh carpets invites us to new and exciting possibilities. By contrast, visit that same place some months earlier when it is a building site and all seems dirt, noise and chaos. At whatever time or place we may visit the church of God on earth we will find more of the building site than the show house. Yet that building is a necessary part of the process, and as we come to the book of Ezra, we are engaging with a hugely significant moment in that long process by which God takes stones from the quarry of this world and gradually builds them into his temple until the house is completed on the foundations of the apostles and the prophets with Jesus Christ as the chief cornerstone.[1] We are at one of the great moments in history and we must not imagine that because the style of Ezra is rather terse that there is not great excitement stirring under the surface.

The book itself falls into two main parts, which tell the story of God's people as they return from exile, setting that story in historical context and forming part of a continuous narrative running to the end of Nehemiah and covering approximately a century. Judah, the kingdom of David, had been brought to an end in 586 BC, nearly seventy years before the book opens. The Babylonians, and the Assyrians before them, transported conquered peoples to new locations in Mesopotamia and planted colonists in the conquered areas. This happened to Israel when the Assyrians destroyed Samaria[2] and to Judah itself when the Babylonians sacked Jerusalem.[3] Now

[1] Eph. 2:19–22.
[2] See 2 Kgs 17:5–6, 24.
[3] See 2 Kgs 25:11.

the Babylonian Empire itself had gone and had been replaced in 539 BC by the Persian Empire under Cyrus. One of the first actions of Cyrus had been to send home the captive peoples who had been brought as exiles to Babylon. So we are now in 538 BC and a party of Judaean exiles have come back home to rebuild their temple. Though the whole book traditionally bears his name, Ezra himself does not appear until chapter 7. The first part of the book (chs. 1 – 6) is a historical survey telling us of the pioneers who returned to Jerusalem some eighty years before Ezra himself. The second part (chs. 7 – 10), sometimes called the 'Ezra memoir', tells of how Ezra himself returned and began a programme of consolidation and reform. We shall find that great skill is shown by the author (probably Ezra himself) in blending the various elements of history, memoir, official decrees, genealogies and prayers into a continuous narrative. The continual allusions to earlier Scriptures give the book a depth and resonance which can easily be missed on a superficial reading.

Ezra is concerned with one main topic – the rebuilding of the house of God – which is also the emphasis of Haggai and, in a different way, of Zechariah. Hence the subtitle chosen for this book is 'Building for God'. However, the temple is gone, and we must not think of such building primarily in terms of bricks and mortar. We are not dealing here with a stewardship campaign or a series of sermons on raising money for the fabric fund. Rather, the concern is for the abiding presence of God among his people who are honouring him by lives as well as lips. The New Testament sees building the temple in terms of living stones growing into a spiritual temple. Thus Paul writes: 'In him the whole building is joined together and rises to become a holy temple in the Lord' (Eph. 2:21). Peter says: 'You also, like living stones, are being built into a spiritual house to be a holy priesthood' (1 Pet. 2:5). The essential point in both Testaments is the presence of God linked in covenant love with his people, anticipating that day when 'the dwelling of God is with men' (Rev. 21:3). It is important to realize that when the Bible speaks of the Lord's 'house' it means the place to which he has come to be with us. Nor is this confined to the temple; Moses is asked to build the tabernacle, which is the place where Yahweh 'will dwell among them' (Exod. 25:8).

1. God takes the initiative (1:1–4)

The Psalmist's words, 'Unless the LORD builds the house, its builders labour in vain' (Ps. 127:1), could be a good introduction to this section. It is, of course, possible to build in the sense of rearing a physical structure, but only if such building enjoys the blessing of the Lord will it fulfil its intended purposes. The subject of the main verb of 1:1, *moved*, is the Lord himself, whose initiative these events are. So the first big theme in this chapter, setting the tone for the whole book, is that of providence. It is true that the word itself does not occur in Scripture, but the idea is one of the great doctrines which flow from the biblical picture of creation. Providence means that God has an ongoing relationship with his creation and directs his creatures and the whole created order ultimately to fulfil his purposes. We need to hold in tension the reality that God works out everything according to his own purposes and yet that humans are responsible beings who are answerable for their decisions and actions. This means that ultimately all human actions, all circumstances and events work together to bring about God's purposes. The classic statement of this in the Old Testament comes at the end of Genesis where Joseph says to his brothers, 'You intended to harm me, but God intended it for good' (Gen. 50:20). The dark background of the brothers' treachery, cruelty and self-interest was woven into a glorious tapestry leading to the fulfilling of God's purposes. We need to remember this when our instant reaction is to ask God to change dark and difficult circumstances rather than, in faith, believing in God's purpose and asking what he wants to teach us. So here, God uses the pagan ruler Cyrus to bring about this next stage in the history of his people. We shall consider this in two ways.

a. Cyrus and the prophets

The phrase *in order to fulfil the word of the LORD spoken by Jeremiah* (v. 1) shows us that providence is not a theory we extrapolate from looking at the world and reading history. God's ways remain opaque unless he graciously chooses to reveal himself. It was not self-evident to the ancient world that the gods spoke and revealed their plans (hence the frantic and fruitless attempt to provoke Baal into speaking in 1 Kgs 18:26–29). But God reveals his plan to his servants the prophets,[4] and that revelation is itself the action of God setting in motion the events which are to come. So we must look at the prophecies of Jeremiah and the references to Cyrus in Isaiah to see exactly what is happening here at the beginning of Ezra.

Ezra, we are told, *was a teacher well versed in the Law of Moses* (7:6), and it is to Scripture that he looks to explain what is happening. The reversal of the exile was no sudden change of heart on God's part but a plan already announced in the prophetic word. Jeremiah 25:1–14 speaks of the nations serving the king of Babylon for seventy

---

[4] Amos 3:7.

years, and in Jeremiah 29:10 the Lord says: 'When seventy years are completed for Babylon, I will come to you and fulfil my gracious promise to bring you back to this place.'[5] When we examine the context of Jeremiah's words in 25:10 we find another fascinating glimpse of God's providential overruling of history: Nebuchadnezzar, like Cyrus, is God's servant.[6] He fulfilled God's plans for destruction as Cyrus would fulfil them for restoration. God's long-term plans for his people are stated in Jeremiah 29:11: '"For I know the plans I have for you," declares the LORD, "plans to prosper you and not to harm you, plans to give you hope and a future."' This is linked in the following verses with prayer and obedience, themes to be important in Ezra.

Ezra is in no doubt that the most important agent at work is the living word of God. We need to recapture that confidence. Above and beyond all the attempts to grapple with postmodernism and exploring new ways of 'being church' we have to believe in the life-changing nature of God's word. More than that, we have to believe that the same word controls and directs history. The words of Jeremiah, which are also the word of God, were the means of exposing pre-exilic corruption and apostasy but now are the means of opening the future and giving new hope. It is hugely important that those who teach, preach and expound the word of God recover confidence in its life-changing power and look to see it do its work.

But there is more than the Jeremiah passages explicitly referred to here, indicated by the use of the verb *moved* – better, 'stirred up' (ESV) – which is what the Lord does to Cyrus' heart. Isaiah 41:2 alludes to Cyrus in the phrase, 'who has stirred up one from the east?' and in 41:25 God says, 'I have stirred up one from the north'. In Isaiah 44:28 and 45:1 Cyrus is named, and in 45:13 is 'stirred up in righteousness' (ESV). Here we see the astonishing precision of God's overruling of history and the amazing exactness with which the living word records this. In Isaiah this is the pinnacle of the entire

---

[5] The seventy years were more like fifty; God graciously shortened the time. There are two other ways we can look at the seventy years. If we take the time as beginning in 605 BC with a small deportation, including Daniel and his friends (Dan. 1:1–6), then it would be sixty-seven years until 538 BC when the pioneers arrived in Jerusalem, near enough seventy. Alternatively, if we take the period from the destruction of Solomon's Temple in 586 BC to the completion of the Second Temple in 516/15 BC we have almost exactly seventy years.

[6] Did Nebuchadnezzar ever become a believer? Dan. 4:34–35: 'His dominion is an eternal dominion; his kingdom endures from generation to generation. All the peoples of the earth are regarded as nothing. He does as he pleases with the powers of heaven and the peoples of the earth. No-one can hold back his hand or say to him "What have you done?"' goes further than his earlier statements.

argument, that God can and does foretell is vividly worked out on the stage of history.

b. Cyrus and the politicians

None of what has been said reduces Cyrus to the level of a puppet. He is issuing his decrees for purposes of his own and establishing a regime very different from the Babylonians and Assyrians who preceded him. We must pause to look at this fascinating man, the conqueror of Babylon and the founder of the Persian Empire. He was the second of that name, usually referred to as 'the Great', who reigned from 559 to 530 BC.[7] It used to be supposed that he was a believer in Yahweh and that he was acting out of a special interest in Judah and its God. However, in 1879 a clay cylinder, usually now referred to as the Cyrus Cylinder, was discovered in the temple of the moon goddess at Ur, which Cyrus repaired. This is a document focusing on Babylon which claims that Marduk, high god of the city, had named Cyrus as its conqueror.[8] It is hardly surprising that the document makes no mention of Yahweh or Judah, but it reflects the policy of allowing people to return to their homelands, mentioning towns across the river Tigris. The Cyrus edict here in Ezra is probably another example of a similar policy, this time tailored to a Judean audience. Moreover, the Persian king was probably casting envious eyes on Egypt, and a grateful population in Judaea would be a fine springboard should conquest be contemplated. It may well be that Cyrus, astute politician as he was, would have in his civil service officials who were well skilled in spin-doctoring and could produce material targeted to specific audiences.

Both prophecy and politics are part of the total picture. The hand of the Lord is at work and what the politicians devise for their own purposes are used by God as he carries out his plans. For Cyrus this was simply another subject people allowed to return to their own land, rebuild their temple and worship in their own way. For God this is part of the great story which began with the creation of heaven and earth and will culminate in a new heaven and new earth. We need to view our Christian work in that light and not be overwhelmed if the establishment try to suppress the church, nor overexcited if the establishment favours it. Both are phases through which God's purpose will be worked out.

The fact that the Cyrus edict is put in writing (1:1) is another illustration of the precision of God's providence. Twenty years later,

---

[7] Ezra speaks of his 'first year' which is reckoned from the time he entered Babylon as a conqueror late in 539 BC.

[8] The Cyrus Cylinder can be read in *ANET*.

King Darius rules in favour of the resumption of the rebuilding of the temple when an Aramaic copy of Cyrus' decree is found in Ecbatana (see 6:1–5). When God wills the end, he also wills the means. Thus Cyrus' words, both oral and written, become the human means by which God's eternal decrees are carried out. This is a view of history we need to extend to all human power, democratic as well as despotic. If, as Paul says in Romans 13:1, that 'the authorities which exist have been established by God' then this is the consistent biblical view and not simply the emphasis of 'the Deuteronomists' or the 'Chronicler' and we can say and sing with confidence 'our God reigns'.

c. Rebuilding God's house

Thus the divine words behind the human words have made possible the launching of this great project to build in Jerusalem a house for *the LORD, the God of heaven.* The title given to Yahweh reflects Cyrus' policy of referring to the gods of other nations the way they themselves did, yet it is also a reminder that this God is not confined to building or country. The title appears a few times in Nehemiah[9] as well as in Ezra[10] and Daniel,[11] emphasizing God's transcendence and his ability to carry out his purposes. He is not confined to one land but is the Creator of heaven and earth.

Why was it so important that the temple should be rebuilt, and why do both Ezra and Haggai emphasize this theme and refuse to let us away from it? We need to look at the central biblical theme of God dwelling with his people. God creates humans in his image to have fellowship with them. Thus in Genesis 3:8 he 'was walking in the garden'.[12] The consummation of this will be in the new heaven and earth where the dwelling of God is with people.[13] However, the fall creates a barrier between a holy God and a sinful people and the flaming sword at the gates of Eden prevent access to the tree of life. After the exodus, God, who in the unfallen world still created a particular place in Eden where he could meet humanity, stipulates that a tent (or tabernacle) is to be made where he will live among his people.[14] The temple is another expression of that conviction and

---

[9] Neh. 1:4–5; 2:4, 20.

[10] 5:11–12; 6:9–10; 7:12, 23.

[11] Dan. 2:18–19, 44.

[12] The verb 'walk' is the Hithpael of *hālak* which has the frequentative sense of habitual walking. This form is also used of Enoch (Gen. 5:22, 24) and of Noah (Gen. 6:9), suggesting that with them God found fellowship.

[13] Rev. 21:3. The nuance must be deduced from the context.

[14] Exod. 25:8.

thus its rebuilding is of crucial importance.[15] The tabernacle and the temple were not just places for holding services but rather the setting for God making his presence known in an unmistakable way. This special presence came to be known as the 'Shekinah' – the dwelling presence which took visible form as a cloud.[16] Yahweh, who had brought them out of Egypt, was to be no absentee landlord but live there among his people.

The temple is linked with the Davidic covenant in 2 Samuel 7 where there is a fascinating wordplay on the term 'house'. David is refused permission to build a 'house' in the sense of 'temple', but the Lord promises to build him a 'house' in the sense of 'dynasty' (2 Sam. 7:11–16). This links the temple with the Davidic line and anticipates the day when David's greater Son will unite heaven and earth to be a temple to his praise.

Probably the passage which shows most clearly both the importance and limitations of the temple is Solomon's great prayer of dedication in 1 Kings 8:27–30. There, Solomon grasps the great twin truths about God which are at the heart of biblical revelation: that God is both 'up there' and 'down here'. These twin emphases are established in Genesis 1 where God the Almighty Creator speaks the universe into being, and in Genesis 2 where he steps down into the world and forms a man out of clay and a woman out of a rib. This is a God who cannot be comprehended but yet is one day to take our flesh. Solomon grasps that God cannot be contained by 'the heavens even the highest heavens' (1 Kgs 8:27) and yet can be met in the temple.[17] This paradox is only to be resolved when the Word takes flesh and leads his people to where there is no temple, for God and the Lamb are there.[18]

Sadly, subsequent history showed that Solomon and many of his successors failed to remain loyal to those twin truths. By building shrines to Ashtoreth, Chemosh and Molech in Jerusalem[19] Solomon showed that he now regarded Yahweh simply as a local godlet. It is worth reflecting too on the story of Joash's abortive attempt to repair the temple.[20] Joash is the patron saint of those who see temple building purely in terms of raising money, running stewardship campaigns and repairing fabric. There is no mention of prayer, of turning to God, of heart engagement, and there is no mention of

---

[15] See further in the exposition of Haggai.
[16] Exod. 40:34–38.
[17] 1 Kgs 8:29.
[18] Rev. 21:22.
[19] 1 Kgs 11:4–8.
[20] 2 Kgs 12; 2 Chr. 24.

Scripture.[21] Contrast all that with the great reforms of Josiah.[22] Josiah's reforms were driven by his desire to serve the Lord without 'turning aside to the right or to the left' (2 Chr. 34:2); his passion for God from his youth; his hatred of idolatry; and above all his obedience to the word of God.[23] His great celebration of the Passover revives and re-establishes godly worship.[24]

Thus here the rebuilding of the temple is a demonstration of how serious the people are to have the Lord living among them.

Comment has already been made on how the temple theme is taken up in the New Testament and on the living stones which are the fabric of that temple. Yet the temple building remains vital throughout Old Testament times. The time has not yet arrived when Jesus is to turn his back on the temple with the words 'your house is left to you desolate' (Matt. 23:38). In John 2:18–22 Jesus makes an explicit comparison between the temple and his body – the true temple – which within three days of its destruction would rise from the dead. His hearers, focusing on the material and temporal, totally misunderstand him. The temple pointed forward to a better and final dwelling of God with his people.[25]

d. Drawing from deep wells

We have already seen how Ezra draws from the pre-exilic prophets Isaiah and Jeremiah. Isaiah 12:3 says, 'With joy you will draw water from the wells of salvation'. This is exactly what Ezra is doing here. In 1:3–4 we have a number of other echoes of earlier Scriptures which reveal the living God meeting with and guiding his people. *Go up* to Jerusalem is an echo of the great pilgrim songs in the Psalter. They recall such words as, 'I rejoiced with those who said to me, "Let us go to the house of the LORD"' (Ps. 122:1). This is a good example of a phrase having both a surface and a deeper meaning: the literal journey to Jerusalem and the spiritual journey which it symbolized. We are not yet specifically to encounter the community at worship, for that we have to wait until chapter 3. Yet here already is being established the priority of praise and service to God and the building of the temple taking precedence over the building of walls and

---

[21] See my 'A Curious Silence: The Temple in 1 and 2 Kings', in T. Desmond Alexander and Simon Gathercole (eds.), *Heaven on Earth: The Temple in Biblical Theology* (Carlisle: Paternoster, 2004), pp. 49–59.

[22] 2 Kgs 22 – 23; 1 Chr. 34 – 35.

[23] See 2 Chr. 34. Read the account of his repentance when the book of the Law is found in 2 Chr. 34:14 –32.

[24] 2 Chr. 35:1–19.

[25] See Rev. 21:2 – 22:5.

houses. The echo of the Psalms, of which Cyrus would be unaware, is another indication of God's providential movement behind the scenes.

Another interesting detail is the word translated *survivors* in 1:4. This word is often translated 'remnant' and we need to look at its theological significance. The word *šĕ'ērît* is a nominal form of *š'r* meaning 'to remain, be left over, to survive', but what is important for our purposes is to see how the word is used to denote a smaller number who are left over from a much larger group and whose existence depends on the mercy of God. It is ultimately through the remnant that God will graciously complete his purposes.

Significantly the first use of the term is found in the flood story: 'only Noah was left (*š'r*) and those with him in the ark' (Gen. 7:23). Through Noah and his family, God's purposes for creation are to be carried on. It is, however, the eighth-century prophets who express the remnant theology most fully. Amos speaks of 'the remnant of Joseph' (Amos 5:15) who are urged to seek God, and before the prophecy of the restoration of 'David's fallen tent' says that the Lord will 'not utterly destroy the house of Jacob' (Amos 9:11, 8). Isaiah also speaks of the remnant in the context of judgment and salvation. In 8:9–22 he sees that the remnant of believing people will not be destroyed, however formidable are the forces arrayed against them, because God is with them. However, that divine security is marked on the human side by a godly lifestyle characterized by faith and obedience and a faith that trusts through days of darkness. Indeed, as the old hymn says,[26] there is no other way but trusting the promises and obeying the commands. We are not here in a world of abstractions but in the true fellowship of the saints, who are chosen before the foundation of the world but respond to God's grace by running the race with patience and perseverance. In Isaiah 10:20–25 the promises to Abraham that his descendants will be like the sand on the seashore will be fulfilled by the return of the remnant from exile. A highway will be opened for the remnant[27] and they will form the nucleus of a new community. The post-exilic prophets identify this 'remnant' with the small group who return from exile.[28] In Ezra itself the word appears again in 9:8, 13–15.

The remnant is thus crucial for the continuity and completion of God's purposes. It is to such a group who are 'waiting for the consolation of Israel' (Luke 2:25), and consisting of people like Mary, Joseph, Simeon and Anna, that the rising sun is to dawn from heaven.

[26] John Henry Sammis (1846–1919), hymn: *When we walk with the Lord (Trust and Obey)*.
[27] Isa. 11:16.
[28] Hag. 1:12, 14; 2:2; Zech. 8:6, 11–12.

So it is at all times of crisis: God's people may be reduced to insignificant numbers but he will preserve them, work through them and move irresistibly to the day when 'a great multitude that no one could count' stands before God and the Lamb (Rev. 7:9).

Ezra is no dry chronicler; in these four verses we have seen wonderful things about how the purposes of God are fulfilled not simply in broad outline but in specific detail. The unity and power of the Scriptures have been demonstrated. God had announced through his prophets both the coming of exile and its ending. We have also seen how Ezra is drawing widely from Scripture to show how God's word not merely says what has happened and is yet to happen, but is also the guide for behaviour in the present. God is still the covenant-keeping God, eager to meet again with his people in the land he had promised to them long ago and to which they now return.

2. The people respond (1:5–6)

Having established that the providence of God and the words of the prophets are behind these events, Ezra now turns to the vital question of the people's response. The more firmly we believe in God's providence, the more eager we will be to be part of his ongoing purposes. Here, as always, the question is whether God will carry out his purposes through his people or in spite of them.

We must look at an important issue here of the priorities of those who returned. It is easy to imagine that exile was virtually synonymous with enslavement and that the whole exiled community in Babylonia were desperate to return home. However, there are indications that for many at least, that was not the case. Jeremiah 29, which consists basically of letters between Jerusalem and Babylon, one from Jeremiah himself, gives us an interesting glimpse of the circumstances of the exiles. Jeremiah encourages the exiles to 'seek the peace and prosperity of the city' (29:7), to build and plant, to take wives and have families. This presumes they were free to do so. Similarly, Ezekiel speaks of their having their own organization with elders, and Ezekiel himself was free to minister to them.[29] Moreover, at least two generations would have grown up in Babylonia who had no personal experience of their former homeland. People with young families and elderly people would be reluctant to face the rigours of a long journey and the return to a broken-down city without amenities and infrastructure. Only a real sense of spiritual priority would have moved even some of the people to return.

[29] See Ezek. 8:1 and 14:1.

All this has great significance for us. One of the great values of the exilic and post-exilic books is that they present God's people in a situation very like our own in the church in the West. In many senses when we think of the increasing weakness of the institutional church, the unbelief in many theological colleges and the ineffectiveness of so many ministries, we are experiencing an exile. The danger, as Malachi powerfully pointed out a generation later, is a deadening apathy and a disdain for God and a complacent acceptance of abysmally low standards. This is a time for an urgent reassessment of priorities and a passionate desire to rebuild the temple of God as the saving gospel is released into the world.

a. A new sense of excitement

The word 'stirred up', already used of Cyrus, is now applied to those who respond to the call to return to Jerusalem and rebuild the house of God. This is emphasized in 1:5; there was no question of rebuilding the royal palace, not even in the first instance the city and its walls, but rather that place which was at the heart of Israel's life and worship. So what were these priorities?

We have already seen that fundamentally building for God is not about bricks and mortar but the realities to which these point. Once again, the words of Jeremiah on the brink of the exile help us here. In his 'Temple Sermon' Jeremiah warns, 'Do not trust in deceptive words and say, "This is the temple of the LORD, the temple of the LORD, the temple of the LORD"' (7:4). The mere presence of a building made with timber and stone in which ritual activities were performed would be no guarantee of God's presence when people were oppressing resident aliens and widows and worshipping Baal.[30] Such 'temple theology' was idolatry and emptied their religion of all validity. But now nothing was more important than to secure the Lord's presence among them and to neglect that sacrament of his presence was to show how little they cared for his presence among them. Jeremiah also reminds the people that no physical structure is sacrosanct, by speaking of the fate of the former shrine at Shiloh.[31] Similarly, Ezekiel envisages the glory of Yahweh leaving the temple, which had become an idolatrous shrine.[32] God was not confined to temples made with hands.

---

[30] Jer. 7:5–11.

[31] Jer. 7:12–15. It was at Shiloh, some twenty miles north-east of Jerusalem, that the tabernacle was placed after the Conquest (Josh. 18:1) and it remained a principal sanctuary during the time of the Judges. The Bible does not give us an actual historical account of its destruction, but excavations on the site reveal destruction, possibly by the Philistines after the battle of Ebenezer (1 Sam. 4:10–11; see also Ps. 78:60–64).

[32] Ezek. 10 – 11.

Yet, as the exiles returned, the physical action of building the temple would be a symbol of their willingness to worship God with their whole lives.[33] Here the association of building the temple with the people's spirits being stirred by God is of a piece with Elijah repairing the altar so that the fire of God could fall upon it.[34] The building of the altar did not bring the fire but it was ready to receive it. The rebuilding of the temple showed that the returned exiles were anxious not only to worship God but to secure his presence at the hear of their community.

We have emphasized that building the church today is about living stones not a physical building. Yet there are times when a fellowship needs to repair, extend or even make a completely new building. If this is because the Lord is stirring hearts, then this becomes an important part of growing the church, as the people pray, give generously and look to extend their mission. If it is simply a job to be done, often backed by dubious fund-raising, then it leads to nothing and is simply repairing a building. Here the initial impetus is the Lord moving people's hearts; later we are to see how this is rekindled by prophetic ministries.[35] Thus the physical action of rebuilding the temple becomes a symbol of willingness to worship God with their whole lives.

This was the generation to which Zechariah spoke words which are most relevant in this context: '"Not by might nor by power, but by my spirit," says the Lord Almighty' (Zech. 4:6). The difficulties already referred to of the journey and the daunting task which awaited the exiles were a real challenge to faith. It is not true to say that difficulties proved the enterprise was of God; such difficulties could also arise from stubbornness, foolishness or inadequate preparation. It is all too easy for some types of Christian to imagine that if something is full of difficulty it must be God's will and for other types to imagine that the absence of difficulties prove that it must be God's will. We need to be open to God's guidance, alert to his word and seek wise advice. Kidner compares this to the whittling down of Gideon's army and later of the crowds in Judaea and Galilee.[36] Gideon needed to learn that God would defeat the Midianites with a tiny handful as well as with great numbers.[37] Jesus withdrew from crowds to solitary places.[38] Yet there are times when large numbers are a sign of God's blessing, as in the phenomenal

[33] See further the exposition of Haggai.
[34] 1 Kgs 18:30.
[35] See ch. 5.
[36] Kidner, p. 34.
[37] Judg. 7:1–8.
[38] E.g. Matt. 14:13.

growth of the early church.[39] This work was to face great opposition but since it was a movement of the Spirit it could not ultimately be stopped.

b. A sense of continuity

We have already noted Ezra's concern to link what is happening here with earlier Scriptures and a similar concern is evident in this section. The first indication of this is that the remnant is further specified as *the family heads of Judah and Benjamin and the priests and Levites* (v. 5). These represented the political and religious leadership and provided real continuity with the pre-exilic nation. It has been suggested that other tribes are deliberately excluded because of their split from the Davidic monarchy in pre-exilic times. That is an unwarranted assumption; this is a matter of historical fact about who actually did return.

It is worth noting that the biblical prophets and historians always see the divided kingdom as an aberration and look to a renewed and reunited kingdom. Two examples will suffice. In Ezekiel 37 the prophet is given a vision of the restoration of God's people. There the reuniting of Israel and Judah is to be marked by God's sanctuary being permanently among them. Similarly, Chronicles is careful to point out that during times of renewal northerners participated in worship at Jerusalem. 2 Chronicles 15:9 speaks of northern tribes joining in Asa's religious reforms, and in 30:11 of those who came to Hezekiah's great passover.

In 1:6 (echoing v. 4) we have another example of continuity with God's acts in the past, this time with the exodus. At that time, there had been the so-called 'spoiling of the Egyptians' where the Hebrews were given silver, gold and other possessions as they left Egypt. Haggai is to say that all the treasures of the nations are the Lord's and, therefore, using them in this way is totally appropriate.[40] Once again there is a link with Isaiah, who sees the return from exile as a new exodus.[41]

The sense of continuity is an essential part of this new episode because the Lord who led the people out of Egypt and now brings them back from Babylon is unchanging. These are acts which reveal his constant faithfulness and thus become the foundation of praise and prayer. Yet hearts must be stirred by the Spirit or the great truths about God will become simply statements held without conviction and without power to stir heart and mind. In such situations, powerful

[39] E.g. Acts 2:41, 47; 6:7.
[40] Hag. 2:7–8.
[41] Isa. 43:16–21; 48:20–21.

prophetic ministries, such as those of Haggai and Zechariah, are needed to call people back to God, as well as Ezra's own prayers and teaching ministry. We need to learn from the past but meet that same living God in the present.

3. The work begins (1:7–11)

When God takes the initiative and his people respond then the actual building work can begin. From here until the end of chapter 2 there are detailed lists of personnel and artefacts and we shall look both at the detail and its underlying significance.

a. Official business

Ezra 1:7 gives a brief summary of the official edict which can be read in detail in 6:3–5. The reference to the sacred vessels is poignant because the last time these had been used was at Belshazzar's drunken feast,[42] but God had preserved them and now they were to be used again in his service.

The two officials who carried out this task are named as Mithredath and Sheshbazzar. Mithredath, a common enough Persian name, means 'Mithras (the sun god) has given'. He is not otherwise known, but there is dispute about the identity of Sheshbazzar. In 5:14 and 16 Cyrus is said to have appointed him governor and it is further stated that he was responsible for laying the foundations of the temple. The problem is that elsewhere (2:2; 3:8; 4:3; 5:2; Hag. 1:1) Zerubbabel is plainly the governor. It has been argued that they are two names for the same person: Sheshbazzar the court name and Zerubbabel the personal one.[43] He is given the epithet 'prince of Judah', and this has led some to suggest that he is the same as Shenazzar (1 Chr. 3:18), a son of Jehoiachin, the exiled king of Judah.[44] Both views have problems; we need to realize that we do not know enough to make a categorical decision,[45] and that the authenticity of the account is unaffected.

b. The furniture of the temple (1:8–10)

The inventory of the temple vessels in verses 9–11 breathes an air of sober reality and authenticity which echoes the loving detail of the

[42] Dan. 5:1–4.
[43] See Dan. 1:6–7 for an example of Daniel and his three friends being given new names.
[44] So Clines, p. 41.
[45] See Kidner, Appendix II, pp. 139–143 for a useful discussion.

account of the building of the Solomonic temple.[46] We read in 2 Kings 25:13–17 of objects plundered from the temple and, as already noted, in Daniel 5. However, here in Ezra is the only occasion on which numbers are mentioned. These numbers suggest the considerable wealth of the pre-exilic temple and, considering the depredations of the four centuries following Solomon, show that scepticism about Solomon's vast wealth is unwarranted. An obvious problem is that the separate items add up to less than the grand total of 5,400.[47] It may be that this list is a selection of the most noteworthy items; there is no mention of the bronze artefacts taken by Nebuchadnezzar. It is also possible that Cyrus may not have returned all the vessels at one time.[48]

What these details do not reveal is the amazing providence of God in preserving these silent tokens of his covenant and endless mercy. One detail, however, is striking because of its absence. Nowhere is the ark of the covenant mentioned, and we need to ask what its absence means. In this ark were the tablets of the Ten Commandments,[49] showing the absolute primacy of the word of God in the lives of God's people. There was also a pot of manna as a reminder of God's gracious provision in the desert, Aaron's rod which budded as a sign that God could bring life out of death, and also validated his priesthood, thus indicating the permanent necessity for a valid priest.[50] The ark was placed in the inner sanctuary where God revealed himself to his servants.[51] It was a sign of God's presence and his glory which 'filled the tabernacle' (Exod. 40:35). Its chequered history included going before Israel at the crossing of Jordan; capture by the Philistines; being placed in the temple by Solomon and relocated there by Josiah.[52] It was central in every sense to the worship of pre-exilic Israel.

Yet Jeremiah warned that one day the ark would be no more and that no replacement would be made.[53] The context is a prophecy of future blessing when God will live among his people and all nations will be drawn to them. Exile is to teach the people that God is not

[46] 1 Kgs 6 – 7.
[47] See Williamson (WBC), pp. 5–8 for a thorough discussion of the list and the various suggested emendations. He is concerned to make the numbers add up and his proposed emendations are trying to do that.
[48] There are a number of uncertainties in the list of vessels. The gold and silver dishes were probably libation vessels and the 'silver pans' (NIV) or 'censers' (ESV) (KJV 'knives') is an obscure word.
[49] Exod. 25:16; Deut. 10:1–5.
[50] Heb. 9:4.
[51] Exod. 25:22; 30:36.
[52] Josh. 3:14; 1 Sam. 4:1–11; 1 Kgs 8; 2 Chr. 35:3.
[53] Jer. 3:16.

locally confined. When Ezekiel sees the vision of the glory of God by the river Chebar, he sees what is, in effect, a mobile ark of the covenant which can travel wherever the Spirit wills (Ezek. 1).[54] This is the chariot throne of Yahweh appearing in Nebuchadnezzar's Babylon and showing his glory in that hostile environment. That glory 'was a figure like that of a man' (Ezek. 1:26). God is preparing them for the day when the true ark of the covenant, the glory of God, is to take the form of a man and live among us.[55] The ark had served its purpose and was probably lost or destroyed when Jerusalem fell in 587 BC. This is yet another example of the providence of God. Had it survived, there would have been a great danger of venerating it for itself, as earlier generations had venerated the bronze snake made by Moses, which was destroyed for that very reason by Hezekiah.[56]

God's glory, however, had not gone and now the exiles have the task of rebuilding the fabric of their lives and restoring the true worship of God in the desolate sanctuary. The phrase *Sheshbazzar brought all these along* is undramatic, but behind it is the sense of this community carrying treasures which they longed to see in their proper place and used for their proper purpose.

c. A turning point

The exiles came up from Babylon to Jerusalem (v. 11) is a laconic phrase but it expresses nothing less than a reversal of the exile, a new exodus and one of the great moments of history. Unlike the exodus story, no details are given of the journey nor of the feelings of those who undertook it. For that kind of story we have to wait for chapter 8 when Ezra himself returns. This is a visible demonstration of the unseen providence of God. This event may not have had the overtly miraculous accompaniments of the exodus but it is no less an act of God. The numbers may be small but they represent the return of the nation and, like their forebears leaving Egypt, they carry gifts from their Gentile neighbours.

Two things can be said. The first is that here we have a blend of international history and the spiritual and personal elements behind it. Cyrus and the Persian Empire are facts of history, and reference has already been made to such artefacts as the Cyrus Cylinder which illustrate the period. Yet behind all this is the prophetic word which becomes actual; we might even say 'becomes flesh' in these apparently mundane happenings. The words of the prophets are

[54] Ezek. 1.
[55] John 1:14.
[56] Num. 21:8–9; 2 Kgs 18:4.

not simply a description of what happens, since they are also the word of God they are the agent which causes these events to take place.

The second is that the eye of faith is needed to see and grasp the meaning of what is happening. This is true in a secondary sense of the reader. Ezra often fails to charm at a first reading, largely because it often seems so low-key and factual. Yet as we look at what is happening and catch the echoes of earlier Scriptures and see the book in the overall biblical picture we realize that God is working his purpose out. Indeed we need such a perception of the way events personal, communal, national and international unfold. Ultimately the Bible's theology of history is that God will be God and the world will know it.

4. Getting our bearings

This short chapter has raised huge issues and done so in a sophistic-ated and deceptively simple manner. As we look to the rest of the book, three observations will help us to get our bearings and continue to learn from the writer.

The first is a literary comment. The author writes in an unadorned and often laconic way and at first sight seems little interested in style. However, he uses language in a rich and evocative way. We have noticed such details as the word 'remnant', the significance of the temple vessels and the echoes of earlier Scriptures. With Ezra we come to a time when probably the earlier Scriptures are being collected and the concept of the Old Testament canon emerging.[57] Thus the words of the prophets are regarded as authoritative and allusions to them in later writings, such as Ezra, come with his full understanding of their whole message. This means that the text of Ezra is rich and multi-layered and builds on earlier revelation, a point we shall return to in a comment on canon. This is no flat and dry chronicle, this pulses with the living words of God.

The second is a theological comment. Ezra emphasizes both the central importance of the temple for the old covenant community and the deeper issues of relationship with God and his presence among them. In that day, the temple vessels were part of the religion instituted by God himself and thus their reverent use mattered. When Paul, in 2 Timothy 2:20–21, speaks of vessels in a large house which

[57] See R. Beckwith, *The Old Testament Canon of the New Testament Church and Its Background in Early Judaism* (Grand Rapids: Eerdmans, 1986), pp. 110–180. We know little of the process, but Beckwith argues that at the end of the Old Testament period, books already recognized as canonical are being arranged into the familiar threefold grouping of Law, Prophets and Writings.

is the church, God's people are the vessels.[58] Just as the temple vessels were sanctified for particular purposes, so the people of God are to be sanctified and offer him spiritual sacrifices.

The temple in Jerusalem, as Ezra and Haggai demonstrate, remained central as a witness to the presence of God among his people. It is not the final destination but it is a stage on the road to the new Jerusalem where there is no temple but the unveiled presence of God and the Lamb.[59] By linking the edict of Cyrus which ordered the rebuilding of the temple with the words of Jeremiah, Ezra has shown that the temple is part of that purpose of God. Through Jeremiah God speaks of people who 'will call upon me and come and pray to me' (Jer. 29:12) and that calling and prayer are given visible expression in the rebuilding of the temple.

The third is a canonical comment. This, along with Nehemiah, Haggai and glimpses in Zechariah, is the only part of Scripture which actually shows the returning exiles. Yet this is a theme addressed in other parts of the Old Testament and these help us to place this episode in its important place in the big picture of Scripture. We shall look at examples of these.

First, there are earlier passages speaking of the Davidic monarchy and predicting its disastrous failure and consequent judgment. God's covenant with David, spoken by Nathan, which we see in 2 Samuel 7, speaks of the eternal nature of God's love and of the Davidic throne and kingdom being established for ever. Yet it also speaks of his descendants being disciplined with 'the rod of men' (2 Sam. 7:14), which includes the exile. This is developed in Psalm 89:38–41 where the Davidic king (presumably, Jehoiachin) finds his 'throne cast to the ground' (89:44). Similarly, Solomon's great prayer of dedication speaks of various calamities which will happen as a result of sin but appeals to the Lord's mercy to restore.[60] What these passages are anticipating is that much of the history of the Davidic line will be marked by faithlessness and rebellion but that God's steadfast love would triumph. What we have here in Ezra 1 is the historical record of these who returned from exile as a testimony to the faithfulness of God.

There is, however, an ultimate eschatological fulfilment and that brings us to another group of passages. These are the passages in many of the prophets which look beyond the exile and see a future which is glorious and transformed. This is a future where

the ransomed of the LORD will return.
They will enter Zion with singing (Isa. 35:10).

[58] See also 1 Tim. 3:15.
[59] Rev. 22:21.
[60] 1 Kgs 8:31–53.

45

This glorious poem looks back to the exodus, which though it involved a journey through a barren wilderness, was the place where God's people saw the glory of the Lord. Similarly the glorious new life will be fulfilled only in the heavenly city. Yet this return of the pioneers to Zion echoed the one and foreshadowed the other. The pages of the Old Testament rustle with expectation: each new king, prophet, each event which aroused hope, seen as evidence that God was fulfilling his ancient promises and would continue his good work.

Similarly, the passage where Ezekiel looks to a rebuilt temple[61] looks back to the exodus narrative and forward to the day of the Lord. The ultimate point is 'Where God is, there is Zion'. As these pioneers returned, their vision was the same as that of Ezekiel; they wanted the presence of Yahweh at the heart of his people.[62]

Perhaps the faith and vision which leads to building for God is best captured in these words by Charles Wesley, echoing Zechariah 4:7:

> Give me the faith which can remove
>   and sink the mountain to a plain;
> Give me the childlike, praying love,
>   which longs to build thy house again;
> Thy love let it my heart o'er power,
> And all my simple soul devour.

Wesley further sees the building of the house as bringing people to the Saviour:

> Enlarge, inflame and fill my heart
>   with boundless charity divine!
> So shall I all my strength exert,
>   and love them with a zeal like thine;
> And lead them to thine open side,
>   the sheep for whom their shepherd died.[63]

Such a spirit will indeed, by God's grace, lead to the building up of living stones in God's temple.

---

[61] Ezek. 40 – 48.

[62] D. I. Block, *The Book of Ezekiel*, vol. II (NICOT; Grand Rapids: Eerdmans, 1998), p. 506.

[63] Charles Wesley, hymn: 'Give me the faith which can remove'.

Ezra 2:1–70
2. What's in a name?

Whatever else we make of this chapter, we must realize that here we are dealing with people who once lived and breathed, who had joys and sorrows and who were far more than the simple chronicling of their names can tell us. The people who returned from exile were no mere anonymous mass and some of them, at least, have their names preserved in Scripture. A chapter like this, however uninviting it may seem, shows consummate planning and has great depth. We shall first make comments on individual issues as they arise, and then say something on the overall relevance and abiding value of the chapter. The list, although many obscurities remain, is clearly presented and Nehemiah was able to use it nearly a century later as part of his organization of the community (Neh. 7:5–67).

1. The list of those who returned

a. Leaders (2:1–2a)

This is seen by some not as a list of returning exiles but rather a composite account of some who returned over a period of twenty years or so.[1] This is unnecessary: the chapter reads more naturally as an expansion of 1:11: *When the exiles came up from Babylon to Jerusalem.* The chapter is rich with echoes of Israel's earlier history and a deep sense of continuity and nationhood which the exile had failed to quench.

The *province* is the old heartland of Judah; in Persian terms only a small part of a larger unit known as 'the province Beyond the River' (4:10, ESV; *Trans-Euphrates*, NIV). Here again is the idea of the remnant, which although small in terms both of people and land is

---

[1] E.g. Williamson, *Ezra, Nehemiah* (WBC), pp. 30–32.

heir to great promises and will enjoy a glorious future. This future is already encapsulated in *they returned to Jerusalem and Judah, each to his own town* (v. 1). At the time of return huge rebuilding projects awaited them of which not a stone had yet been laid, but the account breathes a spirit of hope and new beginnings.

Ezra begins with the names of the leaders of the returned exiles. In the corresponding chapter, Nehemiah (7:7) adds the name Nahamani which brings the list to twelve names.[2] We do not know why the name is omitted here. The number twelve is probably significant as a sign of continuity; this was genuinely Israel which returned. The two leading names are Zerubbabel, grandson of King Jehoiachin, who represents the Davidic line, and Jeshua (Joshua in Haggai and Zechariah), the High Priest (Zech. 3:1). These kingly and priestly lines point to the day when they are to be united in Jesus Christ himself.

The other names in the list are not known elsewhere. Nehemiah is probably not the well-known governor who came later. Likewise the situation at the end of Esther with Mordecai firmly established in Susa as the guardian of his people (Esth. 10:2–3) makes it virtually certain that he is not the same as the man mentioned here. In the ancient world, names were repeated as often as they are today and we need not be surprised that we have both famous and unknown people having the same name.

b. The people of Israel (2:3–35)

The phrase *people of Israel* makes an explicit link with the pre-exilic nation; it is indeed the people of God who are returning. The list falls into two parts: names of families (vv. 3–20) and names by association with home towns (vv. 21–35). Here, in a way we have already seen to be characteristic of Ezra, we have both an obvious and a deeper meaning. The division in the first place probably represents different ways of registering. However, here is also a further fulfilling of the twin promises to Abraham of descendants and land. The sense of continuity throughout the generations and of love for the ancestral land breathes behind this list.

c. The priests (2:36–39)

Only four priestly families are listed here, far fewer than the twenty-four groups David had organized.[3] Yet, as many commentators have

---

[2] The larger commentaries give a detailed analysis of the names, e.g. Williamson, *Ezra, Nehemiah* (WBC), pp. 24–39; Clines, pp. 45–63.

[3] 1 Chr. 24 – 26.

noted, they formed one tenth of the entire group which returned, and were essential for the functioning of the temple. They formed an integral part of the kingdom of priests which God's people were called to be.

d. The Levites (2:40–42)

The *Levites* emerge into prominence in the Pentateuch as the avengers of the Lord's honour after the incident of the golden calf[4] and they have a significant role in the tabernacle, both in its construction and its protection and transport.[5] They had no inheritance in the land but were supported by tithes.[6] What is immediately striking here is that only seventy-four Levites returned. Ezra himself is to discover that no Levites wished to return (8:15).

Various reasons can be suggested for this. It may be that not only, like every one else, they were daunted by the huge upheaval the move would cause but that they had little desire to return to the disciplined and strenuous temple routines. We have a glimpse in Ezekiel 44:10–14 of how some of them, at least, had been ringleaders in idolatry. Ezekiel, however, foresees a day when, after repentance, they will be restored as Yahweh's temple servants, fulfilling the ancient covenant with Levi.[7] It may be that the few who returned here represented a faithful remnant among the Levites.

The *singers* and *gatekeepers* (vv. 41–42) were also of the tribe of Levi, but with specific functions. Chronicles associates the singers with the Levites but it is not altogether clear what the exact relationship was.[8] Nehemiah includes the singers with the Levites but lists gatekeepers separately.[9] The *descendants of Asaph* (v. 41) are associated with Psalms 50 and 73 – 83, one which speaks of being a gatekeeper in the house of the Lord.[10]

e. Other temple servants (2:43–58)

Ezra 8:20 tells us that these people had been appointed by David to assist the Levites. The Hebrew term, also adopted in NKJV, is *nĕtînîm*,

---

[4] Exod. 32:25–29.
[5] Exod. 38:21; Num. 1:47–53.
[6] Num. 18:23–24; Deut. 18:1–4.
[7] Deut. 10:8–9.
[8] E.g. 1 Chr. 6:16.
[9] 11:15–20; 12:24–25.
[10] Ps. 84:10.

which is interpreted in NIV and ESV as *temple servants*.[11] We do not know what particular tasks these people carried out. Some commentators, drawing attention to the presence of foreign-looking names, e.g. Rezin (v. 48) and Sisera (v. 53) and to Jewish tradition which identifies them with the Gibeonites[12] suggest that they were probably little better than slaves who carried out menial tasks. This is not necessarily true because the name could suggest individuals chosen and dedicated for special service. In any case, the people are all being assembled for the supremely important task of building the temple and re-instituting the worship of God. It is not impossible that Paul has in mind the specialist use of *ntn* when he calls church leaders gifts of the ascended Christ to the church.[13]

f. Those of unproven descent (2:59–63)

Tracing descent was important both to establish continuity and to ensure people were who they said they were. More serious was the case of unconfirmed priestly individuals (vv. 61–62). The story of Korah, Dathan and Abiram is a warning of the danger of trying to force a way into the priesthood. 'No outsider, who is not of the descendants of Aaron, should draw near to burn incense before the LORD' (Num. 16:40). We have the sad example of King Uzziah, struck with leprosy for impiously usurping the role of the priests.[14] Nehemiah successfully resists such a temptation.[15]

This process of proper registration of the priestly orders was supervised by the *governor* or 'Tirshatha' (v. 63), a title later used of Nehemiah. This is probably Zerubbabel, who undertakes this task himself at a time before the official order of priests is functioning. The *most sacred food* was the portion set aside for the Aaronic priests.[16]

The *Urim and Thummim* is to be reinstated as the method of discerning the will of God. These two words are normally used together and refer to a means of revelation available to the High Priest. Exodus 28:30 and Leviticus 8:8 suggest that they were two small objects, perhaps gems and kept in a pocket of the high priest's ephod. The use of the Urim and Thummim seems to have died

---

[11] *Nĕtînîm* occurs only in 1 Chr., Ezra and Neh. and is always plural and with the definite article. It is associated with the common verb *ntn*, 'to give'; probably, therefore, meaning those who are given or committed to temple service. A related word, *nĕtunîm*, occurs in Num. 8:16 of the Levites as 'wholly given' to the Lord.

[12] Josh. 9:23, 27.

[13] Eph. 4:7–13.

[14] 2 Chr. 26:16–21.

[15] Neh. 6:10–13.

[16] Lev. 2:3; 7:1, 6.

out after the time of the early monarchy and only revived now.[17] Presumably, if they were flat objects each with a 'yes' and a 'no' side three options were possible. 'Yes' would be two Thummim if related to *tāmam*, 'to be perfect'. 'No' would be two Urim if related to *'ārar*, 'to curse'. No reply would be one Urim and one Thummim. It is probably not the case that they were withdrawn in the later monarchy because of the abundance of prophetic voices, because they were introduced at a time when Moses himself was a present reality. Rather, this reflects the great concern to reinstate everything possible which emphasized continuity and provided a way of access to God.

We must not allow the paucity of some of the information or our uncertainty about the meanings of individual words to obscure the real impact of this passage. The returned exiles, especially their leaders, were determined to be detailed and painstaking in their obedience. As they assembled and planned the work of rebuilding they were anxious to be true to the Torah. In Exodus 25:9 Moses is told to build the tabernacle exactly according to pattern, and the post-exilic leaders are anxious to recover that full and specific obedience as they prepare for God to live among them again. The emphasis here is on a pure authorized community who can carry out the task of rebuilding.

g. The totals (2:64–67)

The total of 42,360 cannot be the sum of the individual totals, which is 29,818 and 31,089 in Nehemiah 7:66. Attempts to explain these discrepancies tend to say that the missing numbers represent women, children and perhaps northern tribes. Probably lists, like genealogies, are selective rather than exhaustive, and plainly in material such as this ancient copyists would easily make mistakes in large lists of numbers.

2. Gifts and settlements

a. The gifts (2:68–69)

The phrase *freewill offerings . . . according to their ability* is echoed in 1 Corinthians 16:2 and is a reminder of the human cost behind all this. Anyone who has moved house knows that in addition to the inevitable upheaval there will be all kinds of extra expenses and many unexpected events. Here this is all magnified by the fact that they

---

[17] 1 Sam. 28:6; see also Neh. 7:65.

returned not to new houses but to a land largely ruined and neglected for nearly seventy years. Yet they gave and did it willingly. It echoes the preparations for the tabernacle in Exodus 25:1–7 and 35:21–29, and for Solomon's temple in 1 Chronicles 29:2–9.

b. The settlement (2:70)

This is a terse summary of what must have been an arduous and complicated business of resettlement and brings to an end the first stage of the return. The actors have assembled, the stage is prepared and the drama is about to begin.

2. Ready for action

No one can fail to be impressed by the detailed and painstaking nature of this chapter. Yet we might feel that there is not much more to be said. If you are not enthusiastic about reading aloud Old Testament passages with lots of names, this is clearly not the one for you. Probably this passage has not featured prominently in the preaching programmes of most churches. Yet God has chosen to give us this and similar passages, and if we take Scripture seriously we must try to explore something of its underlying significance in the ongoing story. Four things can be said.

a. This is part of the great narrative

Dull as it may seem, this chapter is a vital link in the ongoing story from creation to new creation and this can be illustrated in a number of ways. At the beginning the return from exile is underlined, an event which we have seen is of an importance comparable to the exodus. The phrase *whom Nebuchadnezzar king of Babylon had taken captive to Babylon* (v. 1) reminds the reader that the exile had happened and the Lord's people were now returning. Babylon had gone (at least in the old form) but Zion was about to be rebuilt and once again the praise of God would be sung there.

Moreover, the ancient promises to Abraham of descendants and land[18] have not been forgotten. The phrase *each to his own town* (v. 1) suggests a return to places where their ancestors had lived, a resumption of the allocations made under Joshua[19] even if most would have to be rebuilt. 2 Chronicles 36:21 speaks of the land having enjoyed its sabbath rest, but now we enter a new phase and

---

[18] Gen. 12:1–3.
[19] Josh. 13 – 19.

one alive with promise and possibilities. A new era is dawning in the providence of God.

It may be objected that indeed a few exiles did return but the atmosphere is hardly 'the ransomed of the LORD will return and enter Zion with singing' (Isa. 35:10). The prophets do indeed speak in these glowing terms (and we shall return to that), but they also speak in more modest, indeed downbeat terms, of a tiny remnant saved from disaster. Two examples will suffice. Isaiah 6:13 says: 'as the terebinth and oak leave stumps when they are cut down, so the holy seed will be the stump in the land.' Amos 3:12 is even grimmer: 'As a shepherd saves from the lion's mouth only two leg bones or a piece of an ear, so will the Israelites be saved.' Here, in Ezra 2, it is the remnant which has returned, and yet that remnant is the heir of God's promises and from them will come the Messiah. Indeed when the Messiah comes there is only a remnant to greet him, and yet he is the one who will fulfil the aspirations of the returning exiles for 'he will reign over the house of Jacob forever; his kingdom will never end' (Luke 1:33). It is no accident that once again 'everyone went to his own town' (Luke 2:3). This chapter is a vital link in the story and points to the day of ultimate fulfilment when there will be 'a great multitude that no one can count, from every nation, tribe, people and language, standing before the throne and in front of the Lamb' (Rev. 7:9).

All this is most relevant to the church in the West today. In spite of confident prophecies of revival and triumphalist hymnody we are not seeing Zion restored. We face loss of nerve, sheer weariness and the mockery or indifference of the establishment. What are we to do at a time like this? Ezra would say to us that we need to keep on building the temple of God by proclaiming his word so that unbelievers become part of that temple and that those already in it keep on growing; and we need to back that by prayer. A passage such as Ephesians 2:14–22 speaks of the foundation of God's temple on the apostles and prophets, held together by Christ Jesus the chief cornerstone. This often conflicts with the dismal reality of the church on earth and we need to repent and pray and work for its reformation. Being a minority places us where these returning exiles were, and thus the post-exilic books speak directly and powerfully into our situation. Like them we need to be faithful in our time, believing that the promises given to them and fulfilled when Christ came have a yet more glorious fulfilment in the city where there is no temple but where God and the Lamb reign.[20] Most of our names, like most of theirs, are not household words but are written in heaven.

[20] Rev. 21:22.

In Ezra 2 people had to wait for a priest who could consult Urim and Thummim, and living in the fallen world means that we need to accept the limitations of our time and get on with it. At any stage of the story, God is building his temple and we need to carry out diligently the tasks at hand and depend on his faithfulness.

b. We have insights into priorities

This is no random list and the order of the different groups is surely significant. The twelve leaders represent all Israel and they also show the necessity of good leadership in the community. Much of the trouble in old Israel stemmed from bad leadership; often bad kings, some like Rehoboam with bad advisers.[21] Frequently the prophets castigate the leaders.[22] As representing the community they have a particular responsibility and they are the ones whom Haggai is to address first.[23]

But they are leaders because there is still a community to represent: *the men of the people of Israel* (2:2b); and, as already noted, the twin themes of ancestry and land are prominent here. That community, once returned, has as its primary responsibility building the temple. The primary function of the temple was to be the place of the dwelling of God among his people; the fundamental statement of this is first made in relation to the tabernacle: 'have them make a sanctuary for me, and I will dwell among them' (Exod. 25:8). The response to the presence of God among them is the worship of the people.[24] We have already looked at the structure of the list of priests, Levites and *temple servants* and noted the vast importance of all associated with the temple working together and doing their tasks well. Again there is much to learn here and the message is similar to that of Paul's teaching in 1 Corinthians 12 with its emphasis on the organic and mutually-dependent nature of the body. The very compiling of a list like this shows the importance of every individual and every task to the Lord. Few would have realized at first the huge significance of what they were doing but all their contributions were vital.

c. We are a kingdom of priests

The significant role of the priests in this chapter makes this a good place to say something of the significance of priesthood here and

---

[21] 1 Kgs 12:8–11.
[22] E.g. Isa. 1:10; Jer. 22:2–5; Amos 6:1; Zeph. 3:3–4.
[23] Hag. 1:1; 2:2, 21.
[24] See comments on ch. 3.

how that applies to the church as a community of priests under Christ the great High Priest. Plainly priests play a vital role in the establishing of the post-exilic community. A word here on the main functions of the Old Testament priesthood will help to focus our thinking. Effectively they had two main functions. In their liturgical one,[25] they represented the nation to God, regularly bearing the names of the twelve tribes into the Holy Place.[26] Their second function was to teach Torah.[27] A few decades later, Malachi will attack them for failure in both aspects: polluted sacrifices and false teaching.[28] Both elements are vital for the returning community and the priests needed to be very conscious of their responsibilities.

We need now to examine how this applies to God's people today and in particular what priesthood means for us. Already, in the Old Testament, priestly language is applied to the people (notably Exod. 19:6: 'you will be for me a kingdom of priests and a holy nation'). This is taken up 1 Peter 2:9 where it is particularly defined as declaring 'the praises of him who called you out of darkness into his wonderful light'. This complements Peter's earlier idea of offering 'spiritual sacrifices' (1 Pet. 2:5). Thus the whole body of believers is associated with the twin aspects of the Old Testament priesthood. Christ himself is the great High Priest who has gone into heaven and there intercedes for us, and we are priests only in him.

Before Christ the ancient priesthood pointed to him and there were special people set apart to be 'object lessons' of what was to come. Now the whole people of God are priests and all involved in the worship and service of the temple not built with hands. There are, of course, people with different functions, especially teaching ones, but these are not different kinds of people, rather their task is 'to equip the saints for the work of ministry' (Eph. 4:12, ESV). But from Ezra 2 we learn that all need to work together to build the Lord's temple. There is no warrant in the New Testament for applying the name 'priest' to people ordained to certain liturgical functions.

d. The wider context

Ezra and Nehemiah tell us of the return to the homeland and the world of the temple, religious observance and the re-establishing of a lifestyle which will glorify God. Haggai and Zechariah show us the kind of preaching which inspired the returned exiles. Sadly, the

[25] E.g. Ezra 3:10.
[26] Exod. 28:29–30.
[27] E.g. Hag. 2:11.
[28] Mal. 1:6–8; 2:8.

words of Malachi show that a generation later much had been lost, and we already noticed his denunciation of unworthy offerings and false teaching. There is a strong emphasis on Torah. Ezra 7:10 speaks of the importance of the study and teaching of the law, and in Nehemiah 8, Ezra both teaches himself and supervises the teaching of others. The specific role of these books is to show that the exile had not destroyed Israel's faith and that the returned exiles were heirs to the promises of Abraham and of both the Davidic and Mosaic covenants. A chapter such as Ezra 2 with its loving attention to detail and its concern to do things properly bears witness to that.

Yet these books are not the only witness to this time. The book of Esther tells what on the surface is a story of God's people who remained in Persia and appeared to have no wish to identify with the community in Jerusalem. Yet on closer inspection Esther and Ezra/Nehemiah are not as far apart as they might seem. There are, for example, numerous parallels with the exodus narrative – for example when Haman persuades Ahasuerus to proceed against the Israelites, the death edict is issued on the thirteenth day of the final month, which was the eve of the Passover.[29] The stakes are immediately raised; will the God of Israel rescue his people again? Those who did not return are also part of God's overall purpose to preserve the nation from which Messiah is to come. If Haman's plan had succeeded all the nation would have been destroyed, including those who returned to Jerusalem. Behind this is the attempt of the devil to destroy the one to whom the temple points. Esther, no less than Ezra, bears witness to the sovereign God who, working through flawed humans, brings about his purposes, and pointing to the time when the earth will be filled with the glory of God.

Looking at Ezra 2 we can see that it is far more than a list of names. Here we see the community, conscious of a commitment to their roots, yet beginning a new and significant stage in their discipleship. In future chapters we are to see how this works out in the difficult days to follow.

---

[29] Esth. 3:7–14; see Exod. 12:18.

Ezra 3:1–6
3. Getting priorities right

It was R. L. Stevenson who said that 'to travel hopefully is a better thing than to arrive'.[1] These words express admirably the mixed fascination of the journey and what is often an anticlimax when it is over. Here there were special factors which would be an acute pain to the returned exiles. The journey itself would have been difficult, the land had been virtually desolate for decades and Zion itself lay in ruins. There was an urgent need to establish priorities and in doing so to set the whole enterprise on a firm foundation.

The priority was to re-establish the regular worship of God; more will be said about worship but now simply stating the fact shows what is happening here. For decades the corporate life and worship of God's people had been a memory[2] and before the city was rebuilt, before even the materials for the temple were requisitioned, the daily disciplines of worship had to be re-established. There was a determination that this was to be truly scriptural: *in accordance with what is written in the law of Moses the man of God* (v. 2). This is the theme of continuity which we have already seen as fundamental to Ezra's overall picture of building for God.

1. The vital time (3:1)

The *seventh month* was the peak of Israel's year and included many of the most important festivals (Weeks, Trumpets, Day of Atonement, Booths[3]) and thus had enormous symbolic importance. Moreover, the phrase *assembled as one man* is of crucial importance. God had scattered his people in judgment and now is gathering them in mercy. Ezra has emphasized in chapter 2 the importance of the individuals

[1] R. L. Stevenson in his essay, 'El Dorado'.
[2] Individuals kept the faith, e.g. Daniel's windows open to Jerusalem (Dan. 6).
[3] Lev. 23:23–43.

who returned, now he is emphasizing the importance of corporate unity. Plainly, more is involved here than simply lots of people deciding to go to Jerusalem; the Spirit is at work and he is preparing people to build for God. Nehemiah is to use that phrase (Neh. 8:1) of the enormously significant occasion when the people gathered at the Water Gate to hear Ezra expounding the word of God.[4] It was when 'they were all together in one place' that the Spirit descended (Acts 2:1).

2. The vital task (3:2–3)

Once again the laconic style should not blind us to the huge significance of what is happening here. Long ago Abram had set up an altar when he arrived in the land, showing his faith in God's promises.[5] Now his descendants are claiming this land again for God and believing that he will meet them again. A number of issues arise. Again the leadership appropriately takes the initiative but the people are completely behind them and the sacrifices are reinstated.

First of all, it is clear that they wanted to put the altar in the exact place where God had revealed it should be.[6] It is likely that sacrifices had been offered there during the exile (at least in the early days[7]) and that they would remove the evidence of this, which goes far to explain their *fear of the peoples around them* (v. 3). This fear did not prevent them from making their obedience as exact as possible.

The purpose was to sacrifice burnt offerings. The burnt offering was wholly consumed;[8] none of it was eaten by the priests and it symbolized both complete offering of the worshipper to God and the complete acceptance of the worshipper by God. It was the regular offering both morning and evening and at the scheduled feasts. Its purpose was atonement (*lĕkappēr*) and signified the removal of sin so that God's anger was turned away. Here we have an acted parable pointing to the sacrifice of Jesus whom 'God has presented . . . as a sacrifice of atonement through faith in his blood . . . to demonstrate his justice at the present time, so as to be just and the one who justifies' (Rom. 3:25–26). This is at the heart of all true worship because only as we are conscious of grace can we truly serve God. Building for God needs to begin here and to recognize that it is only

[4] Neh. 8:1.
[5] Gen. 12:7.
[6] See 1 Chr. 22:1.
[7] See Jer. 41:5.
[8] See Lev. 1.

by grace that we can stand in God's presence.[9] Further, the altar was a visible sign of the presence and protection of God in the hostile environment, another link with the exodus story.

3. The vital obedience (3:4–6)

This little section is governed by the phrase *in accordance with what is written* (v. 4). It is both simple obedience to a command and also remembering the very heart of their faith and life. The detail is underlined in the use of the words *required* and *prescribed*. The Feast of Tabernacles is described in great detail in Numbers 29:12–38 and the preparations and effecting of such precise regulations would take great care and precision. In all seventy-one bulls, fifteen rams, 105 lambs and seven goats would be required. It was one of the great pilgrimage-festivals lasting seven days, from the fifteenth to the twenty-second of the seventh month, and every male was required to appear.[10] This was the festival celebrated by Solomon at the dedication of the temple and was part of Hezekiah's reformation.[11] It is also referred to as 'Booths' or 'Succoth' and 'the Feast of Ingathering' (Exod. 23:16) or simply 'the Feast' (John 7:37).

Celebrating this festival now, at the time of return, is charged with huge significance. It reminded the people of the desert wanderings: 'so that your descendants will know that I had the Israelites live in booths when I brought them out of Egypt. I am the LORD your God' (Lev. 23:43). It was an occasion of great rejoicing and thanksgiving and associated with the blessings of harvest.[12] In a vivid way the festival brings together the great Old Testament themes of creation and salvation. In the bounty of the harvest the goodness of the Creator can be seen and celebrated.[13] The visible reminder of the desert wanderings is a tribute to Yahweh who brought them out of the land of Egypt. Now at this new beginning, the returned exiles reaffirm their faith in the Lord of creation and history.

A number of reflections arise from this. First, the exiles were celebrating the faithfulness of God. The ancient promise that seed-time and harvest time would never cease is again being demonstrated.[14] Likewise they were back in the land and beginning a new phase, indeed a new settlement, after a new exodus. A great cloud of witnesses was indeed surrounding them at this moment.

[9] See Heb. 10:19–22.
[10] Exod. 23:14–17; 34:23; Deut. 16:16.
[11] 1 Kgs 8:65–66; 2 Chr. 30.
[12] Deut. 16:13–15.
[13] Ps. 65:9–13.
[14] Gen. 8:22.

Second, they had painfully learned the vital importance of obedience. Disobedience had led to exile and fulfilled the curses of Deuteronomy 28:15–68. That lesson had been learned, at least for the moment, but it is a lesson that God's people need to learn and keep on learning in every generation that obedience needs to be detailed and faithful to the word of God.

Third, this renewal of worship points beyond itself. The God of creation and history is Lord of the future. The exodus commemorated at tabernacles is a trailer for that greater exodus also to be accomplished in Jerusalem.[15] The harvest points to God's kingdom coming at the end of the age.[16]

This is followed (v. 5) by the regular pattern of sacrifices, sacred feasts and freewill offerings. *Burnt offerings* have already been commented on; they formed the regular daily diet.[17] The *New Moon sacrifices* were monthly and the *appointed sacred feasts* seasonal. Here is still a good rhythm: regular so that we worship 'seven whole days, not one in seven',[18] and special so that the regular does not become mechanical. Moreover, *freewill offerings* shows that not only what was prescribed but what expressed gratitude was part of their worship. Deuteronomy 16:10 says that such a gift ought to be 'in proportion to the blessings the LORD your God has given you'. Thus it is a love offering which is inspired by the love of the Giver himself. So the returned exiles are practising the means of grace and beginning the reconstruction of the community.

Verse 6 acts as an *inclusio*[19] with verse 1 and emphasizes the beginning of a new era starting on the day which began the climax of Israel's year, heralded by trumpet blasts.[20] The temple building has not yet begun but it was important to begin those activities for which the temple existed.

4. Worshipping the living God

This chapter raises many important issues relating to worship and we need to reflect further on these, particularly on how they throw light on current debates. We shall outline current issues in perception of worship and see how this passage helps us to think them through.

---

[15] Luke 9:31.

[16] Isa. 52:7–12; Zech. 12 – 14; Matt. 13:39.

[17] See Num. 28:1–8.

[18] George Herbert, poem, 'King of glory, King of peace', 1633.

[19] *Inclusio* is a literary term describing how the beginning and end of a section is indicated by using the same or similar words in both cases.

[20] Lev. 23:24.

Today we find two polarized positions. One view associates worship purely with events which happen in church buildings. The question 'where do you worship?' will be answered by naming a church building or other meeting place. Within the church service worship is more particularly associated with singing. If a church has a 'worship leader' we can be certain that such a person leads the musical part of the service. It is common, especially in university towns, to hear students say that a particular place is great for worship and another for teaching. In any Christian bookshop, books on worship will normally focus on the event of being gathered in church and 'worship CDs' will be songs. Such a view will draw heavily on Old Testament language and will speak of temple, praise, sacrifice and the emphasis on singing, especially in the Psalms.

The other view emphasizes that the whole of life is worship, and their answer to the question 'where do you worship?' will be 'wherever my body is', citing Romans 12:1. At church services, commonly called 'meetings', the emphasis is on encouragement, teaching and training; singing will often be a minor item. Indeed, it seems that the only place we do not worship is when we meet together. This view points to the use of temple language in the New Testament where it refers to people not places and to the absence of 'worship' language in the few places where the early church meetings are mentioned.[21]

Both views contain truth and error and what is needed is a healthy biblical balance. Ezra 3 provides guidance on a true biblical theology of worship.

a. True worship is controlled by God's word

The first thing to say is that true worship is controlled by the word of God. We do not have in the New Testament the detailed regulations which governed Old Testament worship (many referred to in the earlier discussion of these verses), but we must not infer from that that our worship is to be less biblical. Two points can be made. The first is that truly biblical worship now that we have the complete canon of Scripture will have the reading and exposition of the Bible at its heart. Nehemiah 8 is to show Ezra involved in just such an exposition of earlier Scripture. The second is that true worship needs to draw on the great biblical doctrines of creation and history which we have seen to be at the heart of the celebrations in this chapter. With the coming of Christ these great truths shine with greater clarity but they flow continuously from Old Testament times.

[21] E.g. 1 Cor. 14; Heb. 10.

b. True worship is God-centred and in fellowship with others

True worship is both God-centred and sensitive to others; it will have both transcendence and immanence. Five times in a few verses the name Yahweh appears, and carries with it all the mystery and majesty of the revelation to Moses in Exodus 3. Meditating on that name not only recalls God's past faithfulness but his present grace and promise for the future. Once again, with our knowledge of the Lord revealed in the Word made flesh, the honouring of that Name which is above every name will have deeper dimensions as we worship the One who sits on the throne and also the Lamb who was slain.

Yet this worship is not solitary: *the people assembled as one man* (v. 1) and as well as praising God they had fellowship with each other. Also, the emphasis on Moses and their continuity with him show that they were also part of a greater fellowship across the ages. This is wonderfully expressed in Hebrews 12:22–24:

> You have come to Mount Zion, to the heavenly Jerusalem, the city of the living God. You have come to thousands upon thousands of angels in joyful assembly, to the church of the firstborn, whose names are written in heaven. You have come to God, the judge of all men, to the spirits of the righteous made perfect, to Jesus the mediator of a new covenant, and to the sprinkled blood that speaks a better word than the blood of Abel.

What happens here in the ruins of Jerusalem, with an altar raised in the yet unbuilt temple, is part of that same great story. Every gathering of God's people on earth, however unpropitious the surroundings, anticipates the day when the complete company which no-one can count gathers around the throne in the city where a temple is no longer needed.

c. True worship has both a daily and a special rhythm

True worship has a rhythm which is both at the heart of daily living and focused at special times. We have noticed how the daily burnt offerings reminded the people that worship involved everyday living. This is as much a truth in the Old as in the New Testament. The Psalter is full of such a consciousness. Psalm 92:2 speaks of proclaiming God's love in the morning and his faithfulness at night; Psalm 1 speaks of continual meditation on the Torah; Psalm 19:1–2 speaks of the daily witness of the heavens and Psalm 119:164 speaks of praising God seven times a day. It is vital for the returned exiles to re-establish these daily patterns and live the whole of their lives as living sacrifices. For the church today it is also vital to live lives of worship which will include, but not be confined to, whatever patterns of Bible reading and prayer we practise.

Yet, for this daily worship to be more than simply repeated actions there must be special times when the worship of daily living is focused in a particularly rich and evocative way. Here it is the great Feast of Tabernacles which provides such an occasion. We have already seen the powerful associations of this festival and its dramatizing of the great centralities of Israel's faith. In a real sense all worship, all life, is special, but until we reach the city where work and worship are one we will need special times and places. If I say I can forget my wedding anniversary or my wife's birthday because I love her all the time, you would conclude either that I was a dull dog or that the life had gone out of the relationship. So it is with our relationship with the Lord; our daily walk with him needs times when we focus on him and his great love and mercy.

d. The presence of God is crucial to true worship

Fourth, there is the relationship between the temple as the place where God revealed himself and the provisional and temporary nature of the structure. This offering of sacrifice began *though the foundation of the LORD's temple had not yet been laid* (v. 6). One thing we can dismiss instantly is sentimental attachment to buildings which are regarded as 'temples' or 'houses of God' and where such buildings are seen as linear descendants of the temple. We have already seen that the temple in the New Testament is the body of Christ; first his own body, which is the expression of the glory of God, and then his people indwelt by the Holy Spirit. However, we need to realize the central importance here of the temple (as we shall explore further in Haggai) and its importance for us in emphasizing the presence of the Lord at the heart of his people.

Here two important principles are established. The first is that the altar comes before the temple. The establishing of obedient and orderly worship showed that they were determined that the temple would not be the idolatrous shrine from which the glory of Yahweh had departed.[22] The second is that the rebuilding of the house of the Lord shows that his glory has again come to live with his people. It was a sign that they were serious about God being amongst them. The lesson for us is underlined by Paul when he speaks of

[22] Ezek. 10.

the gathered church exercising the gift of prophecy and says that in such circumstances the unbeliever 'will fall down and worship God, exclaiming, "God is really among you!"' (1 Cor. 14:25). When priorities are right, building for God will surely follow and that is what we consider next.

Ezra 3:7–13
4. Starting to take shape

In a real sense what has happened up to now is preparatory to the task of building the temple of the Lord commissioned by Cyrus (1:3) and provided for by the freewill offerings of many heads of families (2:68–69). We move now to the beginning of the actual work on the structure and the mingled feelings of those who were involved. It is important that we examine what is happening here so that we do not fall into the mistake of some commentators and find a contradiction between this and Haggai 2:15–18 which also mentions the laying of the foundations.

We have already considered the important implications of altar coming before temple, and before examining the detail of this passage we must look at what the author means by the foundations of the temple being laid (v. 10, echoing v. 6). The verb used here and in Haggai 2:18 is *yāsad*. This certainly can mean laying the foundations for the first time[1] but can also mean various stages in a process. As we shall see, when Haggai comes twenty years later the abandoned foundations would have to be reworked and strengthened. Thus there is no contradiction, rather, a lengthy building project is implied.[2]

However, the emphasis on foundations is more than a technical point about the range of meaning of a word. The foundations of a building are essential for its long-term stability. The author of Hebrews speaks of Abraham's faith as he looked for the city which has foundations.[3] These foundations are a result of the city being designed and built by God himself. The New Testament temple is

---

[1] As in 1 Kgs 5:17.
[2] For further discussion see A. Gelston, 'The Foundations of the Second Temple', *Vetus Testamentum* 16 (1966), pp. 232–235; Andersen.
[3] Heb. 11:10.

built on the foundation of the apostles and prophets.[4] Here the foundation is more than the stones in the ground, it is the Torah and the obedience of the earlier verses which form the spiritual foundations. We shall look at the story in three stages before making some comments on the passage as a whole.

1. Echoes and memories (3:7)

Our author has already shown his deep familiarity with earlier Scriptures and his ability to evoke echoes which link this work with God's continuing purposes. Two things in particular call for comment. The first is the echo of Solomon's preparations for the temple. In 2 Chronicles 2:10–16 we read of how timber was sent from Joppa and payment made by wheat, wine and oil. This allusion does not mean, as some have said, that this is fiction modelled on the earlier account. Rather the similarities show a consciousness that this work, like the earlier, is a practical demonstration of the peoples' desire for God to live among them. The new factor here was the authorization by Cyrus, a reminder that they were no longer an independent nation but, like Phoenicia, a province of the Persian Empire. There is no starry-eyed dreaming here; this is the reality of life under the Persian Empire.

Yet that is not the whole picture. The other echo is of Isaiah 60:13:

> The glory of Lebanon will come to you,
>   the pine, the fir and the cypress together,
> to adorn the place of my sanctuary.

That passage is particularly significant, echoing Solomon and anticipating the rebuilding. Yet it anticipates far more than this, as can be seen in the other reference in Isaiah to the 'glory of Lebanon' (Isa. 35:2) which looks to nothing less than the new heaven and the new earth. Thus this apparently low-key restoration is a significant link in the big story and a guarantee that God is working his purpose out. We shall find a similar emphasis in Haggai 2:6–9.

Thus we have a blend of sober realism and joyful anticipation here which will always be characteristic of building for God. We will use the means to hand, receive the permission we need but yet be conscious that it is God's work and its final outcome more glorious than we can imagine.

---

[4] Eph. 2:20.

2. Leading the process (3:8–9)

The link with Solomon's temple is again underlined because it was in the second month that the first temple had been started.[5] The first month was dominated by the Passover. Verse 8 is interesting for the striking phrase, *after their arrival at the house of God in Jerusalem*. Some argue that this refers to a later period because the author is much more concerned to keep a typological connection with the Solomonic temple and because it would take a considerable time to bring the timber from Lebanon.[6] That is unnecessary. The whole purpose in returning was to rebuild the house of God and thus to bring the Lord once again right into the heart of where his people lived. Yet we have seen that in another sense he could be met already by obedience and sacrifice. Moreover, the permission of Cyrus had already been given and much of the preparation may already have taken place.

The emphasis here is on leadership and united efforts in the project. Once again, the Davidic line is represented by Zerubbabel and the priestly by Jeshua. The high standards set and the attention to detail continues both in the appointing of workers and the supervision of the work. Twenty may seem young to be in a supervisor's role but we have to remember the relatively small numbers available and the importance of youth in the long-term project.[7] Such things are also true, especially in pioneering Christian work, today. The emphasis on the Levites is an echo of 1 Chronicles 23:24 where David organizes them in preparation for the building of the first temple.[8]

The importance of leadership in supervising the building is underlined. The spelling out of the names, the care in appointing supervisors and the repetition of the word *supervise* (vv. 8–9) show that this was no hasty and random selection. As with the festivals, meticulous care marked all the preparations. That will always be a feature of true building for God and will be the necessary background for the more important things which follow. Similarly, the emphasis on unity (*joined together*, v. 9) echoes Psalm 133 about brothers living together in unity.[9] The builders have assembled, the materials are ready and the time for building has come.

[5] 1 Kgs 6:1.

[6] See e.g. Williamson (WBC), p. 47.

[7] Num. 8:24 speaks of twenty-five and older, and Num. 4:3, 23 and 30 of thirty to fifty. Plainly, the circumstances would determine the pool of labour available.

[8] *The sons of Henadad* are not mentioned in 2:40, although they do appear in Neh. 3:18, 24; 10:9. This is another reminder of the selectivity of lists such as those in ch. 2.

[9] It is worth noting that in Ps. 133:1 'living together' and 'in unity' are not identical. The use of the word *gam* ('also') shows that it is a shared purpose, not simply propinquity, which brings about the blessing of the Lord's presence.

3. Praise and nostalgia (3:10–13)

This is a remarkable section both bringing to a close the preparatory material thus far and giving some pointers to the future. A great ceremony had marked the dedication of Solomon's temple,[10] and something similar when Hezekiah later cleansed the temple.[11] Work was still at an early stage; only the foundations had been laid but it was a time for praising God. Yet the Davidic and Solomonic echoes continue to emphasize continuity between the worship of post and pre-exilic times.[12] *As prescribed by David king of Israel* (v. 10) parallels *what is written in the Law of Moses the man of God* (3:2) and links what is happening with the great figures of the past. The vestments and the instruments reflected the desire for everything to be done well and faithfully.

But the emphasis here is on what was sung and we shall look at both elements: praise and nostalgia. Here the deep emotions of worship and praise which have run deeply now well up to the surface. Two words encapsulate the moment; related but not identical. They sang with *praise*, the word *hālal*, which echoes through the Psalter culminating in the great paean of acclamation which is Psalm 150 and is a response to who God is and what he has done. It is the true response to God's covenant faithfulness. *Thanksgiving* more specifically relates to their own awareness that they owed their preservation and safe return and the work of rebuilding so far to the grace of God. What they sing is a refrain which occurs more than once in the Psalms.[13]

The word *good* (v. 11) is not simply a vague term of approbation as it tends to be in English. This is the word which runs through Genesis 1 and speaks of the pleasure of the Creator as he rejoices in what he has made. Creation reflects the perfection of the one who made it and what is good is what fulfils the purpose for which it was created.

The word translated as *love* (NIV) and 'steadfast love' (ESV) is *hesed*, which is specifically God's love shown in the covenant. At its heart is a relationship where the faithfulness of God evokes a response of faith in humans. The divine love is characterized by unchanging faithfulness in spite of the poverty and fickleness of the human response, as is evidenced by the people here and the movement to rebuild the temple. This is underlined by the words *to Israel* which

---

[10] 1 Kgs 8; 2 Chr. 5 – 7.

[11] 2 Chr. 29:25–30.

[12] See 2 Chr. 5:12; 7:6.

[13] See Pss 100:4–5; 106:1; 107:1; 118:1, and 136:1, where the latter phrase is repeated throughout the psalm.

is now, at least as a remnant, returned to the land of the covenant. This psalm fragment then expresses publicly the feelings which have been present in the text but not made explicit until now.

The praise is enthusiastic. The word *těrû'â* (v. 11) can be a *shout* of victory in war and is associated with the cry of acclamation when David brought the ark of the covenant to Zion.[14] Here the building of the temple will signify the return of Yahweh to his city. Perhaps the use of this particular word draws attention to the victories of Yahweh the Warrior who, as already noted, has initiated this new exodus.

But praise is not the only note which sounds in this remarkable scene. Weeping among the veterans who had seen the first temple breaks into the chorus of praise. It is not entirely clear why the old men wept. Much depends on whether we see this as part of the overall praise with the weeping being tears of joy rather than sorrow.[15] The probability is that they were disappointed and rather than entering the spirit of praise gave way to nostalgia for what had once been. This is the beginning of the spirit of defeatism which is to be condemned by Haggai[16] and it is to be a continuing problem as the work progresses.

The scene is fascinating in its realism. *No one could distinguish the sound of the shouts of joy from the sound of weeping* and the emphasis is on the great noise. It is not immediately obvious why this detail is included but it may be that apart from the actuality of the account the author is showing that even a community who had *assembled as one man* (3:1) were already showing tensions.

4. Further observations on building the temple

Since we shall not return to the building of the temple until 6:13–15 and then only to look at the completion of the project, it would be useful here to make some further comments on the significance of the temple in the life of Israel and reflect on its contemporary application. For the returned exiles the temple is the visible sign that Yahweh has returned to his land. Three things can be said about its significance.

a. The temple is the visible sign of God dwelling among his people

This meant first that its rebuilding was essential because not to do so was a statement that God's presence was an optional extra (more

---

[14] Ps. 47:5.
[15] The *waw* probably is better taken in the sense of 'but', 'however' which would underline the contrast between the praise and the weeping.
[16] Hag. 2:3.

of this in Haggai). Yet there was the opposite danger that the outward appearance of the building would become more important to them than the reality to which it bore witness. This is reflected in the nostalgia for old, far-off things which mingled with the rejoicing. So far all had gone well and the sacrificial system had been reintroduced with meticulous care, but the work had to be completed.

The song they had sung (v. 11) showed their commitment to the true worship of God. However, as we are all aware, it is relatively easy to sing songs of praise and mean what we sing but show less enthusiasm for building these truths into our lives. How seriously these words were meant was about to be tested and the building of the temple was to become less of a priority. This meant that worship and obedience would also become lesser priorities. Since the praise of God for all times and all places was especially centred on the temple as it had been in the earlier tent it was a focal point for God's people as they travelled from all parts of the land and later from the diaspora.

b. The temple is a powerful link with God's mighty acts in the past

Particularly with a Davidic king no longer on the throne, the temple is more needed than ever. In exile, when there was no possibility of temple, then the spiritual reality was still there, and we see this most obviously in figures such as Ezekiel and Daniel. The temple is a reminder of the faithfulness of God from the time of the exodus until now. We have already noticed the many powerful links with the past and this tangible sign is the visible embodiment of the faith of generations.

Today we need vivid reminders of God's faithfulness in the past and his presence working powerfully among his people. This, for us, is not buildings but the word of God and the record of his blessings throughout the centuries.

c. The temple is a reminder that the story is not over

There is a provisionality to the temple as there was earlier to the tabernacle. They both belong to the era which the author of Hebrews describes as 'an illustration for the present time' (Heb. 9:9). Hebrews also speaks of the heavenly temple which already exists and is the prototype of the earthly one.[17] This is also underlined in Exodus 25:9, 40 where Moses is told to follow the pattern revealed to him on Sinai. David, likewise, in 1 Chronicles 28:19 speaks of the

---

[17] Heb. 8:2; 9:24.

details of the temple which the Lord had revealed to him. Thus, the earthly temple points forward to the future as well as echoing the past. It stands between the original meeting of God with humans and the dwelling of God with them.[18] This means that the temple is regarded with the utmost seriousness yet can never be seen as an end in itself.

The fact that John's vision in Revelation sees no temple in the city[19] is not a contradiction of Ezekiel's vision of the restored temple[20] but rather a different vision of the same reality, which is God's presence among his people in a new heaven and earth. This is underlined by Revelation 21:3 where the tent of God is with mortals. The object of both tent and temple was that God could live in the midst of his people, and the thrust of Ezra 3 is that the returned exiles, at least for the moment, recognize this and are striving to create the conditions where this can happen.

5. Getting our bearings

These first three chapters of Ezra have established a number of important facts and given us guidelines for interpreting the rest of the book. Three comments will help us as we move on to the next part of the story.

The first is the sense of a great communal endeavour. Admittedly the overall numbers may have been relatively small but this remnant is continuous with pre-exilic Israel. From it will come the Messiah whose life, death and resurrection will secure the destiny of the great multitude no one can count and fulfil the ancient promise that Abraham's descendants would be like the stars in number. This sense of corporate identity is to be important throughout the book, though we are to see threats to it as the early enthusiasm wanes in the face of opposition, and the later corporate repentance. However, those who argue that leadership is less significant in this period than at earlier times ignore the importance of Zerubbabel and Jeshua and later Ezra, not to say the prophetic ministries of Haggai and Zechariah.[21]

The second is the emphasis on altar and temple before the rebuilding of the city. The priorities are made clear: sacrifice and repentance

---

[18] Gen. 3; Rev. 21:3. See the interesting chapter by Crispin Fletcher-Louis, 'God's Image, His Cosmic Temple and the High Priest', in T. Desmond Alexander and Simon Gathercole (eds.), *Heaven on Earth: The Temple in Biblical Theology* (Carlisle: Paternoster, 2004), pp. 81–99, where he argues that tabernacle and temple are a mirror image of creation.

[19] Rev. 21:22.

[20] Ezek. 40–44.

[21] See e.g. Dillard and Longman, pp. 210–211.

is to be at the heart of their way of life. Idolatry and unbelief had led to the exile, these must not be repeated; even before Ezra returns to expound the Torah, there has been a strong emphasis on doing what Moses commanded. Thus God sends prophets and a teacher so that the work can be built on strong spiritual foundations.

The third is the underlying emphasis on the providence of God[22] and the sense that something significant is happening. The purposes of God are being fulfilled, overruling and indeed working through the policies of a pagan monarch, the apparent dead wood of lists of names and the first stones laid in the rebuilding programme. This will be essential when we come to chapter 5 where that providential care seems to have receded and the work begun with enthusiasm to have ground to a halt.

[22] See the exposition of ch. 1.

Ezra 4:1–24
5. The vultures gather

Those who have worked extensively with young people, and not only with young people, will know that great enthusiasm and early promise is often followed by a rapid cooling off and a waning of the initial excitement. So it is here. Up to the end of chapter 3, with the exception of the reference to the *fear of the peoples around them* (3:3) and the possible negative note in 3:12 and 13, all has been progress, obedience and rejoicing. But now the work is to come to a stop for twenty years and we are shown why this happens. Two preliminary matters are of some importance before we look at the chapter in detail.

1. The structure of chapter 4

Some argue that the structure of this chapter owes more to literary than historical considerations because the main section (vv. 6–23) deals with the city walls rather than the temple.[1] However, this is not necessary, because we are moving into a situation where from now until the end of Nehemiah there is to be continual opposition to the building of both the temple and the city. So here in chapter 4, to help to explain what follows, we are given a sample of one of the letters of complaint sent to the Persian court, and, as we shall see, this is a particularly comprehensive and virulent letter which well illustrates the nature of the opposition the people faced.

The structure would then look like this:

vv. 1–5:   The beginning of the opposition.
vv. 6–23:   The nature of the opposition.
v. 24:   The results of the opposition.

[1] See Williamson (WBC), pp. 56–60.

2. The inevitability of opposition

The work of God in the world is never an easy and interrupted progress. The significance of the events of chapters 1 – 3 is a sign that God is continuing his purpose and fulfilling his ancient promises. Thus opposition is going to be fierce and sustained and people need to be ready to deal with it. We need to appreciate the deadly nature of this opposition or we shall fall into the trap (not always avoided by commentators) of seeing the resistance to it as narrow and petty. We shall also see the multi-faceted nature of the opposition and the ingenuity of the opponents.

3. The beginning of the opposition (4:1–5)

Significantly, the new actors in the drama are described as *enemies*, which alerts the reader instantly to the true issues at stake. Probably they are the same as *the peoples around them* (v. 4, and 3:3), more exactly *the peoples of the land*. They are not further defined, except that they claim to be descendants of those deported by Esarhaddon. 2 Kings 17:24–41 speaks of deportations from Babylon and elsewhere to replace those taken into exile on the fall of Samaria. However, this appears to have been a continuing policy of the Assyrians.[2] What is more important for our purposes is to examine how this opposition begins and see in it a window into how such hostility always attempts to destroy God's work. Three different techniques are used.

a. We're all in this together

The first kind of opposition seems like a friendly gesture which the returned exiles rebuff rather rudely and apparently sanctimoniously. An offer of help is made, but Zerubbabel and the other leaders summarily reject it (v. 3). We have to ask what is actually at stake here. We are not dealing with minor and secondary issues, rather with the very heart of the gospel: who God is and how he is to be worshipped. This is not a question of people agreeing on fundamental biblical truths and having differences on secondary matters. What is being proposed here is in fact a multi-faith act of cooperation.

The key again lies in 2 Kings 17. When Sargon of Assyria resettled Samaria with colonists from Babylon and elsewhere we are told,

---

[2] Texts from the reign of Esarhaddon speak of removing people from the east to Sidon, and it may well be that similar deportations happened during his Egyptian campaigns in 673 and 671 BC (see *ANET*, pp. 291ff.). See also Isa. 7:8 where the sixty-five years after the Syro-Ephraimite war would bring us to Esarhaddon's Egyptian invasion.

'When they first lived there, they did not worship Yahweh; so he sent lions among them and they killed some of the people' (v. 25). Subsequently, one of the exiled priests was sent back to Bethel to teach them how to worship Yahweh. This proved ineffective as verse 33 shows: 'They worshipped Yahweh, but served their own gods.' The purely superficial nature of their worship is demonstrated by their failure to 'adhere to the decrees and ordinances, the laws and commands that Yahweh gave the descendants of Jacob' (v. 34). Basically they are returning to the syncretism of Jeroboam, son of Nebat[3] and repeating the idolatrous behaviour which led to the depopulating of the land in the first place. Thus, whatever claims their descendants make, they are not worshipping God but a collection of local godlets.

Now, the building of the temple showed the desire of the people to bring the presence of God back into his city. Therefore, to 'worship' with the people of the land would be to bring back the idolatrous practices which had caused the Lord's glory to leave the temple.[4]

So this is not narrowmindedness or rudeness, but a conviction that God is to be worshipped in the way he ordained rather than in ways which suit us. Doubtless, since imperfect humans were involved, some would have political motives, but this does not mean that the refusal was political.[5] Nor does it mean that for there to be cooperation in the work of God that participants must agree on every detail. Rather there must be shared loyalty to the gospel and not the attempt to reduce everything to the lowest common denominator. Building for God can be done only on the foundation of the apostles and prophets as living stones are added to God's temple, and anything which obscures that in favour of a vague and sentimental religiosity must be given the same response as here. Gospel work can only be done in the name and for the glory of Christ.

b. Continuing discouragement

Blandishments and flattery failed, so the opponents of the work try another tack – persistent discouragement.[6] This is couched in general terms but the next section is to give a specific example of the kind of opposition they faced. The general effect of all this is to sap the will of the builders. Part of it is sneering and intimidation and part

---

[3] See 1 Kgs 12 – 14.
[4] See Ezek. 10.
[5] This is the view of Blenkinsopp, p. 106.
[6] The verbs in vv. 4–5 are participles which suggest continued and prolonged harassment: *měbahălîm*, 'dismaying'; *sōkěrîm*, 'hiring', 'bribing'.

of it is bribery to get them on the wrong side of officialdom. We have already seen how meagre was the actual visible evidence of the temple building, only the foundations at this point, and we are to learn from Haggai that this external pressure was matched by a growing internal reluctance and defeatism.

Essentially what is at stake here is distinctiveness. Israel was called to be a holy people and a light to the nations. This meant resistance to anything which diluted the Torah and failed to conform to its standards. Such battle is to be fought in every generation, not least in a world of multi-faith, of syncretism and widespread biblical ignorance.

4. The nature of the opposition (4:6–23)

If there was any doubt about the virulence of the opposition this long parenthesis makes very clear the nasty and deadly nature of the attack. We have here a 'flash forward'[7] showing that this opposition continued during the reigns of Xerxes and Artaxerxes and giving an example of a letter written to the Persian court.

a. The setting

The *accusation* is dated in the reign of Xerxes (Ahasuerus) and the *letter* in the reign of Artaxerxes. Xerxes (486–465) is the king who is at the centre of the events in Esther and the successor of Darius (v. 5). The reason for the accusation is not given[8] and nothing appears to have come of it. However, in the following reign, that of Artaxerxes (464–423), the complaints become more specific and have more effect. This letter is the second one (assuming that the *accusation* of v. 6 was in the form of a letter) but we are not given the text. It is written in Aramaic, the lingua franca of the ancient Near East, and indeed, the next passage from 4:8 to 6:18 is in Aramaic (as is 7:12–26).[9]

The third letter, whose text is to follow (vv. 11–16), is introduced by a roll-call of names to make it sound sonorous and impressive. This is probably why *as follows* at the end of v. 6 is not followed by the text of the letter but by the list of officials and their provinces. But we turn to the underlying thrust of the letter, which shows the nature of the opposition and the tactics employed.

[7] The phrase is used by McConville, p. 25.
[8] Some commentators link it with a rebellion against the Persians in Egypt with which the people of Judah were – or alleged to be – sympathetic. See Clines, p. 76 and Williamson (WBC), p. 60.
[9] A similar change to Aramaic occurs in Daniel 2:4 to the end of ch. 7.

b. Exaggerate your own importance and marginalize your opponents

Rehum and his associates are clearly out to impress Artaxerxes both with their own importance and the assertion that they speak for the overwhelming majority. This is the establishment flexing its muscles and attempting to intimidate by sheer force of numbers and the display of pomp and circumstance. This time (unlike in vv. 1–5) they are going over the heads of the exiles and attempting to use the law to force them into line. They further describe themselves as the men of 'Beyond the River' (v. 11, ESV; NIV *Trans-Euphrates*) who speak for the whole province. The designation is originally geographical and includes the land west of the Euphrates as far as the Mediterranean including Judah and Samaria; it was one of the provinces of the Persian Empire. The returned exiles are seen as a small minority out of step with the consensus and, although dangerous, ultimately insignificant.

So it is today. The media regularly sneer at the church, using tendentious words such as 'fundamentalist' and decry and denigrate all those who speak for gospel values as a tiny and fanatical minority. It needs a firm faith in God and the unseen realities to stand against such pressure and misrepresentation.

c. Rewriting history

This is done in two ways: whitewashing the enemies of God's people and misrepresenting the people and their history. It is a clever blend of tendentious opinion, manipulation of facts and plain exaggeration, and calculated to appeal both to Artaxerxes' sense of importance and play on his fears.

First the whitewashing of God's enemies. We have the astonishing phrase *the great and honourable Ashurbanipal* ('Osnappar', in Aramaic). This is the Assyrian king who ruled 669–627. The specific occasion of his deportation of the current complainants' ancestors is unknown, but it is known that he quashed rebellions in Babylon and Elam and it is probable that he could have uprooted people from there and sent them westwards. But what is significant is the epithet *honourable*. Ashurbanipal was the last of the strong Assyrian kings; fifteen years after his death Nineveh was destroyed and the Assyrian empire with it.[10] It is further interesting to note that the horrors of deportation are glossed over and the event spoken of as if it were merely an administrative detail.

---

[10] Ashurbanipal was a bloodthirsty tyrant who continued the militaristic policy of his predecessors, sacking Thebes in 663 BC (mentioned in Nah. 3:8–10).

Secondly, this letter misrepresents the history and intentions of the returned exiles. This is the substance of verses 12–16 and takes a number of forms. The first question, however, is to decide who are *the Jews who came up to us from you* (v. 12). This does not necessarily imply that they had just returned; *from you* could simply mean from Persia. The issue turns on what is meant by the phrase translated by the NIV as *restoring the walls and repairing the foundations*. Plainly the walls were far from finished and we do not have the detailed evidence to tell us exactly who this group were; they may have been the people who came with Ezra himself in 458 BC, or perhaps a later group, In any case, this kind of hostility, as we have seen, is characteristic of the whole period of return and rebuilding.

The complainers begin with a general condemnation of *that rebellious and wicked city*. This is the kind of vague and generalized statement which is used to create a mood rather than give real evidence. The complainers are relying on a mixture of their own prestige, the far-flung nature of the empire and the suspicions of the king to stop the building.

First they allege (v. 13), without any supporting evidence, that the community would not pay taxes. This is given a semblance of veracity by mentioning three different kinds of revenue: taxes, which would be monetary; tribute, which would probably be in kind, and duty, which was probably a kind of toll. They also represent this as a personal affront to Artaxerxes: *the royal revenues will suffer*.

Then they grovel and display sycophantic loyalty (v. 14). It is difficult to see this as genuine concern for the king, rather they are looking to their own interests and hoping that such ultra loyalty will be rewarded. This is shown by urging the king to look in the state archives for evidence of earlier rebelliousness. The *archives of your predecessors* would probably not simply be the immediate predecessors of Artaxerxes but would go back to Babylonian and Assyrian times (as in the earlier reference to Ashurbanipal). Such matters as the rebellion of Zedekiah and the defiance of Hezekiah would be there. The whole thing is presented with great exaggeration. The idea that a rebellion in a small province would threaten the whole empire is ludicrous.

d. The juggernaut of the law

Exaggerated or not, the accusations worked, probably because they appealed to the king's own insecurity and self importance. He responds with a letter of his own (vv. 17–23) which gives the complainants what they ask. Even the great days of David and Solomon are used against them.[11] Thus the king uses the law to stop the building work in Jerusalem. However, he leaves his options open to rescind this at a later stage (v. 21). He does not authorize the opponents to demolish the work, simply to halt it, which they do forcefully and no doubt with alacrity.

5. The results of the opposition (4:24)

This verse takes up the story from verse 5 and shows that the work which had been 'frustrated' was in fact halted for twenty years until the deadlock was broken in the second year of Darius. The phrase *came to a standstill* is deeply depressing and many must have felt that this was the final curtain rather than a temporary setback. However, the description of the temple as *the house of God in Jerusalem* carries its own story; it has all the implications noticed in chapter 1 and is a reminder that God's purposes cannot be stopped.

6. General comments

What we have in Ezra 4 is one of the most significant biblical pictures of how opposition to God's work arises and apparently triumphs and it would be useful to look at how this remains of continuing significance.

a. God's work will always encounter opposition.

The chapter is an illustration of Paul's words in 1 Corinthians 16:9: 'A great door for effective work has opened to me, and there are many who oppose me.' The 'and' is significant; the fact is that God's work attracts opposition. There is, of course, opposition which arises from our own stubbornness and misguidedness, but that is not what is happening in 1 Corinthians 16 or in Ezra. This is opposition to God's work and an attempt to thwart his purposes. Our Lord warns his disciples of hardships to come: 'They will treat you this way

---

[11] Some commentators argue that even in the days of David and Solomon, the phrase *ruling over the whole of Trans-Euphrates* would have been an exaggeration and see it as propaganda. However, recent research shows that 'mini-empires', including those of Israel, were characteristic of the 12th to the 10th centuries BC. See K. A. Kitchen, 'The Controlling Role of External Evidence in Assessing the Historical Status of the Israelite United Monarchy', in V. Philips Long, D. W. Baker and G. J. Wenham (eds.), *Windows into Old Testament History* (Grand Rapids: Eerdmans, 2002), pp. 111-130.

because of my name, for they do not know the One who sent me' (John 15:21). Throughout the book of Acts periods of growth are paralleled by periods of persecution.

This calls for realism and endurance. Building for God will never be easy and enjoy uninterrupted progress and setbacks will often come to test our commitment. Here it is more than simple trials; this is an attempt to hijack the return to Jerusalem of the indwelling of God among his people.

b. Opposition will take many different forms

We need to be on our guard because we do not know what form it will take. Here we have flattery, lies, bribery, appeal to the law and the use of force. Both the variety of these methods and their cumulative effect are deadly. We have here the impression of a war of attrition where people's nerves are worn down. It is not so much an all-out brutal attack as a steady wearing down of resistance which results in a weakening of resolve and a state of apathy such as is implied in Haggai 1. A remarkable comment on this soul-destroying apathy occurs in a commentary on Zephaniah by George Adam Smith: 'The great causes of God and Humanity are not defeated by the hot assaults of the Devil, but by the slow, crushing, glacier-like mass of thousands and thousands of indifferent nobodies.'[12] Vivid language (and we shall meet the 'hot assaults of the Devil') but conveying powerfully the sheer debilitating nature of sullen and sustained indifference and the wearisome grind of continually failing to find encouragement. All who live the life of faith will know of such times. Thus we see the need for perseverance and for a sober realization that the long haul will be more testing than the short, if intense, conflict.

c. We need to recognize the source of the opposition

An important clue occurs in verse 6. The phrase *they lodged an accusation* is more sinister than it appears. The word translated *accusation* is *śiṭnâ*, a form of Satan the adversary. What we have here is another example of the great battle first announced in Genesis 3:15 where the Lord announces the undying hostility of the serpent to the people of God. This is what Ephesians 6:11 calls 'the devil's schemes'. Just as in Esther, where he uses the malevolence of Hanan and the megalomania of Xerxes to try to wipe out the whole people,

---

[12] G. Adam Smith, *The Book of the Twelve Prophets*, vol. 11 (Aberdeen University Press, 1928), p. 52.

so here he uses accusation and discouragement to hinder building for God. So we must know our enemy.

d. See opposition as part of the big picture

The previous comment has underlined the ultimately satanic nature of the opposition and this is compounded by the apparent silence and absence of God. The work, we are told, *came to a standstill.* This is a situation the devil loves; if he can trap us into believing we are in a cul-de-sac we will lose heart and stop building. In such circumstances we need to take our stand on God's earlier assurances, not least the praise of 3:11: *He is good; his love to Israel endures for ever.* This is a God who does exactly what he promised, at the precise moment he promised it and in face of all the odds. When we come to an apparent graveyard of our hopes, we need to renew our trust in a God who knows his way out of the grave.

Ezra 5:1–17
6. God's work cannot be stopped

The last chapter ended in an atmosphere of gloom and pessimism and of a story ended abruptly when it had hardly begun. But God is always surprising our pessimism by his complete relevance and infinite resourcefulness. Sixteen years have passed since the start of rebuilding in chapter 3 and apathy and lethargy now prevailed. When that is the case, a powerful new impetus is needed to cause people to wake up and start effectively living and working for God again. So it is here.

1. The living word (5:1–2)

Before building restarts and before the leaders reorganize, the word of God comes through two prophets. The original impetus in chapter 1 was from the words of Jeremiah, now Haggai and Zechariah come with the word which brings life. The differences between these prophets are well known but should not be exaggerated.[1] Both brought the message they were given and both had key parts to play.

We must look at what specifically they had to say. Haggai we shall discuss fully later, but plainly he is addressing the lethargy and apathy which the opposition of chapter 4 had produced. He exposes the basic attitude which fails to see that only in the present, rather than in some ill-defined future, can the work of God be done. 'These people say, "The time has not yet come for the LORD's house to be built."' (Hag. 1:2). He also castigates the attitude which shows no diminution of enthusiasm for personal comfort and private lives but no enthusiam for the house of God. 'Is it time for you yourselves to be living in your panelled houses, while this house is a ruin?' (Hag. 1:4). He

---

[1] 'Haggai the plain speaker, who dots every "I", while Zechariah is provokingly enigmatic and visionary', Kidner, p. 53.

further urges specific effort: 'Go up into the mountains and bring down timber' (Hag. 1:8). Haggai realizes that while there is real external opposition, the inward will must be captured and then that opposition will be faced.

Zechariah emphasizes the Lord's commitment to Zion: 'I am very jealous for Jerusalem and for Zion' (Zech. 1:14). He underlines the dwelling of God in his city: 'Sing and rejoice, O daughter of Zion, for behold, I come and will dwell in your midst, declares the LORD' (Zech. 2:10, ESV). For that to become a reality at this time, the temple must be rebuilt. It was indeed a 'day of small things' (Zech. 4:10) and the reality of the situation in Ezra 5 made the claims of glory seem over the top, yet by rebuilding the temple they were preparing the way of the Lord and being a vital link in the final coming of the kingdom.

Such preaching had an effect and the civil and religious leaders begin work again. Two phrases are to be noted which bear on both the work of God and human responsibility. The first is *the God of Israel, who was over them* (v. 1). This is a reminder that since the work is God's it cannot ultimately be frustrated. The second is that *the prophets of God were with them, helping them* (v. 2). The nature of the help is not specified but plainly would involve encouragement, further giving of God's word and general moral support. The sword of the Spirit was being wielded with powerful effect.

Here we have the vital place of the preached word in any building for God. This is not the first time we find such emphasis. In 1 Samuel 3 the Lord raises up Samuel to unleash his word on that appallingly degenerate society.[2] In 2 Chronicles 34, the discovery of the Book of the Law provides the impetus and sustaining power for Josiah's great reformation.

So it is now; no lasting work for God can be done without the word of God being both its origin and continuing inspiration. We can thank God for the growth of expository ministries in the post Second World War period and the parallel burgeoning of evangelical scholarship. But this is something every new generation needs to learn, for without this we are becalmed in the shallows of chapter 4.

2. The official response (5:3–6)

The atmosphere of verses 1 and 2 has been so different from chapter 4 that we could easily forget that outwardly nothing had changed. The opposition remained and had not changed their minds. What had changed was the transformation of the people's hearts by the living word of God. What we have here is probably nervousness on

[2] See Judg. 17 – 21.

the part of the officials rather than malevolence, although probably they were informed of the progress of the temple building by its opponents. The first two years of Darius are known to have been unsettled with many local revolts, and in such circumstances provincial governors would understandably be nervous. Tattenai appears to have been subordinate to a higher official[3] and thus would be doubly anxious to appear loyal and efficient.

This was no perfunctory inspection. They not only demand to know the builders' authority, but even a list of names. There is abundant scope here for mischief making. However, this is very different from the beginning of chapter 4 because *the eye of their God* was watching over them and that means that he would oversee the completion of the work. This overruling will be seen clearly in the next chapter in the letter of Darius. The silence of God had not meant the inactivity of God.

3. A significant letter (5:7–17)

The tone and atmosphere of this letter is very different from the one in chapter 4 and presents the reply of the Judaean leaders without tendentious glosses. It begins with a fair summary of the local officials' inspection (vv. 8–9). Problems have been found in the expression *the temple of the great God* (v. 8), but it could simply mean the chief god. The officials were probably unaware of the monotheism of the leaders.[4] The account is brief with factual touches such as the timber, usually understood as helping to strengthen buildings against earthquakes. Further they present the reply of the leaders without comment. The narrative gives no hint as to whether Tattenai and Shethar-Bozenai were more sympathetic to the building project or simply being diplomatic. That does not matter. Because the eye of God was supervising the enterprise, the difficulties are being removed.

The reply of the Judaean leaders in verses 11–16 is full of interest, and a number of significant points are made. Verses 11 and 12 are a concise summary of their history with important theological weight. We shall look at these in turn.

a. The assertion that God is the Creator

We have already come across the title *God of heaven* (1:2) but here we have the addition *and of earth*. This recalls the language of

---

[3] Tattenai was governor of Trans-Euphrates but was under Ushanti in Babylon. See e.g. Clines, pp. 84–85.

[4] Although Clines argues that the expression could mean 'the great house of God' (p. 86).

the Psalms: 'My help comes from the LORD, the Maker of heaven and earth' (Ps. 121:2). Similarly, the reference to Solomon's temple recalls his great prayer where he recognizes that even the highest heavens could not contain God, yet asks that he may look with favour on the temple.[5] This God is the universal Lord and is not confined to a locality. Thus the building of the temple is linked with the great reality of the Creator who graciously reveals himself there.

b. God is Lord of history

But if he is such a great God, why has he allowed his temple and city to be destroyed? Here we have the theology of the exile[6] that God handed his people over to Nebuchadnezzar as a punishment for their rebellion. Once again we have a great deal of Old Testament theology encapsulated. Amos had castigated Israel, warning them that their covenant status, far from protecting them from judgment would make it more severe.[7] Likewise Jeremiah in his temple sermon warns against trusting in outward appearances.[8] Now the exile has happened and the words of God's prophets has been fulfilled.

Likewise God had used Cyrus to reverse the exile and to authorize the building project. We have already discussed the temple vessels and the possible identity of Sheshbazzar in the exposition of chapter 1, but it is worth noting that again the sense of continuity with the first temple is being emphasized. Here we have the conviction that God is Lord of history allied with practical good sense in that the key role of Cyrus is emphasized to the present king.

c. God's concern for detail

The early part of the letter to Darius shows the conviction that God is in charge of creation and of the sweep of history. Thus the emphasis on the name of Sheshbazzar and the care of the vessels complements the big picture, showing how this is worked out in small details. This is further underlined by the request (v. 17) to look for Cyrus' decree in the royal archives of Babylon.

---

[5] 1 Kgs 8:27, 29.
[6] Also in Dan. 1:2.
[7] Amos 3:1-2.
[8] Jer. 7.

4. The broader picture

We shall now look at the chapter in terms of where it fits into the broader picture both of the book of Ezra itself and the whole sweep of God's purposes.

a. This chapter breaks the deadlock

The events recorded here give us a glimpse of how at several levels significant happenings are moving the story forward. On the spiritual level, the preaching of Haggai and Zechariah restores the commitment and morale needed to resume the work of building. On the political level, the apparent goodwill, or at least neutrality, of Tattenai and Shethar-Bozenai had provided a more hopeful environment. On the diplomatic level, the words of the Jewish leaders were a model of courtesy and tact. All these played a significant part and all were used by God in different ways to bring about his purpose. We need to remember that God works in a great variety of ways and uses all kinds of agents and methods. So it always is with all significant works of God. They flow from Scripture and those stirred by the word work out the practicalities in the world.

b. It suggests that God is at work behind the scenes

The words of the prophets are a sign of that, and there is also a fascinating glimpse of this in Zechariah 3. There the prophet shows us Joshua, the High Priest, standing at the altar with Satan at his side to accuse him. Satan's opposition, as we have seen, lay behind that of the Samaritans in chapter 4. But God intervenes and rebukes Satan and, most significantly, is described as 'The LORD, who has chosen Jerusalem' (Zech. 3:2). This means that no demonic opposition, official antagonism or human inertia can prevent the building of the temple and the restoration of the city. Nor can these prevent the completion of God's purpose when the temple of God, composed of every believer throughout all the ages, is presented to the Lamb in the new creation. When we read Ezra 4 – 6, seeing behind it all the hidden purposes of God, we can see that even at this outwardly unpromising time his eternal will is being worked out. We can read the book of Esther in that way as well and see how all the machinations of leaders and the imperfections of God's human instruments cannot prevent God's plans happening.

c. It shows a sense of the events in the bigger context

We have already seen how verses 11 onwards deal with big theological truths which have the effect of showing how the rebuilding of the temple is part of God's overall purpose. The Lord who made heaven and earth is committed to his people, as the summary of some of the salient facts of their history shows. Not once, throughout the book of Ezra, are we allowed to forget that this low-key restoration is the work of God and an essential link in the chain.

d. It shows the need for faith

The letter sent here could have been sent twenty years before; the difference this time was that Zerubbabel and Jeshua found courage and took the risk of being rebuffed or worse. There is never a time when doing what is right is easy. Faith and human action are not incompatible with the providence of God; indeed they are the way in which the will of God leads people to work out his purpose. At this time only the foundations of the temple were laid and the prospect looked as bleak as possible. This faith is seen in taking the risk of beginning to work again and believing that God would honour what they did.

e. The necessity of the preaching of the word of God

God's way of breaking the deadlock is not initially the political moves of Tattenai and Shethar-Bozenai and the response of Darius. Rather it is the unleashing of the word of God which breathes life into the ashes. Without that everything else would ultimately have been a failure. The sending of Haggai and Zechariah is hugely significant in at least three ways.

First, this links the present enterprise with the words of God through Moses which led to the building of the tent in the desert. When we read Exodus 25:9, 'Make this tabernacle and all its furnishings exactly like the pattern I will show you', we have the word of God setting out the place and conditions in which the Lord will live among his people. The prophets are raised up by God to turn the people back to the words originally given to Moses and to re-establish true covenant living with God in the midst. This has been one of the great themes of the book, the continuity of God's purposes.

Second, the words of the prophets, while continuous with and faithful to the words spoken long ago by Moses, are also new words coming into this new situation. These words have authority because they are spoken *in the name of the God of Israel* (v. 1) and thus cannot be ignored. As we shall see in the exposition of Haggai, the prophet echoes earlier Scripture throughout but consistently presents that word in his own context.

Third, the message remains relevant for every age. The early tabernacle, the various earthly forms of the temple, and the living temple of God's people throughout the ages are all born 'not of perishable seed, but of imperishable, through the living and enduring word of God' (1 Pet. 1:23). Thus the prophetic message is an essential part of our being built up in the temple of God. We have noticed the phrase about the prophets *helping them* and as we try to build for God these same prophets are part of the help God sends us. This chapter has much to say to those who find building for God tedious and unproductive, and will give renewed confidence in the power of the living word to break down barriers.

Ezra 6:1–22
7. The king and the King

The dynamics of this chapter are best grasped when we compare 6:1 and 6:22. The chapter begins with an action of Darius who appears to be in complete control of events, and on the surface that is true. However, the phrase *King Darius then issued an order* is balanced by the statement that it was the Lord who changed his attitude (v. 22). Here again we have this characteristic interplay of providence and human responsibility which is at the heart of the book of Ezra. And here we reach the end of the first part of the book, the times of Zerubbabel and Jeshua.

The theology of the chapter is reflected in its style, with the blend of the official language of decrees and the language of worship and celebration. There is an atmosphere of authenticity about this chapter which is important. This is real history about actual people and events. Yet the sense is also one of the fulfilment of God's purposes and the completion of an important stage of the work. Here we have two kings at work. The king of Persia proposes in the outward scene and the King of heaven disposes behind the scenes. The chapter falls rather neatly into three parts: Darius authorizes the work (vv. 1–12); the temple is completed (vv. 13–18); the Passover is celebrated (vv. 19–22).

1. Decrees new and old (6:1–12)

Events now move fairly quickly as Darius mobilizes the civil service to search for the scroll containing the original decree of Cyrus. A note of authenticity is struck with the mention that the scroll was discovered in Ecbatana, which was the former capital of Media. We know also that Cyrus stayed there during his first summer after his conquest of Babylon,[1] the year in which he issued the decree.

---

[1] E. J. Bickerman, 'The Edict of Cyrus in Ezra 1', *JBL* 65 (1946), pp. 249–275.

Probably what follows is an extract from a longer document which concerned matters other than the temple and its vessels. This first section of the chapter falls into two sub-sections.

a. Past royal actions (6:1–5)

Here again we have two agendas working. Cyrus was not specially favouring the Judaeans, rather they were simply part of his policy of *glasnost* for all religions.[2] Yet these verses are full of hints, in a way we have come to see as characteristic of Ezra, that God is at work and another reminder of the significance of what is happening.

The first hint is the phrase *as a place to present sacrifices* (v. 3). Some commentators see this as a rather pointless phrase;[3] but it is an echo of chapter 3, and more than that, a reminder of the whole covenantal relationship on which this enterprise is built. Indeed in chapter 3 the sacrifices began as soon as the altar was built and before the temple foundations had been laid. Priorities are to be observed, and the decree of Cyrus speaks more wisely than he knew.

The decree next specifies the dimensions of the temple. Once again Cyrus is making sure that his precise instructions are obeyed. Some have objected that he would not have known or been interested in the dimensions of the building, but that is unrealistic. It is not likely that Cyrus would have been given vague instructions about the rebuilding of a temple of which he knew nothing; he would doubtless have (or his officials certainly) discussed the details with the Judaean leaders. The payment from the royal treasury (see v. 8) would emphasize the imperial support for the repatriation and re-establishment of worship and would probably come from provincial rather than central revenue.

The reference to the vessels brought by Nebuchadnezzar to Babylon is a reminder both of the divine punishment which was the exile and its divine reversal. The echo here of Daniel 1:1–2 underlines the providential nature of the whole sequence of events. The further detail – 'each to its place' (v. 5, ESV) is a further underlining of the importance of detailed obedience which was emphasized in chapter 3.

b. Present royal decrees (6:6–12)

As Kidner points out,[4] what happens here is the best possible scenario. The work is given royal support and finance but there is

---

[2] The Cyrus Cylinder speaks of the images of the gods of Sumer and Akkad being returned to their temples, Cyrus Cylinder lines 33–36, *ANET*, p. 316.

[3] E.g. Clines, p. 91.

[4] P. 57.

no interference. Here we have an extract from the letter Darius sent to Tattenai and the other provincial leaders. Darius' instructions are negative – *do not interfere* – and positive – provide all that is needed. Again there is clear evidence of Darius listening to the Judaean leaders in the comments he makes. The details of sacrificial animals (v. 9) is a case in point.[5] He also requests prayer for himself and his family. Even more remarkably, he sees that the temple is the place God dwells not by an image, but by his Name – his essential revealed nature.

The savage punishment for tampering with the edict (v. 11) is recorded without comment. We need to compare this with such events as the destruction of the conspirators against Daniel who themselves were devoured by lions.[6] Often, in this world, God's judgments are shown in allowing the law and other agencies to take their course.

The edict ends with a command that the work be done *with diligence*. It is interesting that Haggai was saying similar things, and another reminder that behind the decrees of the king stood the purposes of the King. This word *diligence* is picked up in the beginning of the next section (v. 13) and is to be its keynote.

2. Finishing the work (6:13–18)

This section begins with noting that Tattenai and Shethar-Bozenai gave full support. At this time the civil powers are helpful and constructive (we have already seen the opposite). Such conditions need to be accepted as a gift from God and used to further his work, and here is part of his gracious providence to bring this project to completion.

What is more interesting is the powerful theological undergirding of this section. We are emphatically shown that this is no mere use of favourable circumstances but a demonstration of how God worked, and indeed what is true of all times when he is at work. The Lord has worked on the heart of the king and the officials but he is also working at a far deeper level. Four things call for comment.

a. The preaching of Haggai and Zechariah (6:14)

This is again identified as a major cause of the renewed efforts. Haggai 1:12 states that the whole impetus to complete the building was spiritual: 'they obeyed the voice of the LORD their God and the

[5] See Exod. 29:38–41; Lev. 2:1; Num. 28:1–15.
[6] Dan. 6:24.

message of the prophet Haggai, because the LORD their God had sent him. And the people feared the LORD.' Haggai would clearly be aware of the political machinations but ultimately these are unimportant in comparison with the word and fear of the Lord. Zechariah had emphasized that God's work needs to be done in God's way: 'Not by might nor by power, but by my Spirit, says the LORD Almighty' (Zech. 4:6).

Moreover, we have again a link between the words of kings and prophets. We saw in chapter 1 how the words of Jeremiah and the words of Cyrus were both agents of God's purpose. This did not mean that both were inspired but that the words of Cyrus, all unknown to himself, were used to fulfil the divine word spoken through Jeremiah. The mention here of Artaxerxes (v. 14) has been regarded by many as an insertion because the temple was completed in 516 BC and Artaxerxes belonged to the following century,[7] but that is to miss the point. It was under Artaxerxes that the city walls were completed and thus he, along with the earlier kings, is another human instrument used by God. He is the king who is to give the commission to Ezra himself (7:11) and Ezra's mission is to continue building the temple, not in the sense of its physical fabric but of its spiritual significance.

The linking of the words of the prophets and these three kings has another significance. The old argument about whether prophets were 'foretellers' or 'forthtellers' continues to get an airing from time to time. Liberal scholarship has always tended to see the prophets as speaking to their own day and seen alleged glimpses of the future as either written after the event or simply more or less inspired guesses. Here the prophetic word could be read simply as urging the people to get on with the task in hand. But that is to take too narrow a view. Of course the prophets speak to their own time and penetratingly expose the spiritual and social conditions. Yet the reason why they have such relevance not only to their own times but to every time is that they speak from an eternal perspective. Because their ultimate vision is of the day of the Lord they speak to the whole sweep of history (hence here the mention of Artaxerxes) and speak an authoritative word into every situation.[8] Thus their words are part of God's contemporary word to us as we in our day are involved in the building of God's house.

That word is here specifically linked with the completion of the temple *on the third day of the month Adar, in the sixth year of*

[7] E.g. Clines, p. 95; Fersham, p. 92.
[8] Almost certainly both Haggai and Zechariah have said many things not recorded in their books. Similarly some of the things there might not have formed part of their oral ministry, especially the later parts of Zechariah.

the reign of King Darius (v. 15). Adar, the last month of the Israelite year, was probably late February to mid March, just before the Passover, and the sixth year of Darius would be 515 BC. God's timing is precise and its recording accurate.[9]

b. The great celebration (6:16)

This follows the completion of the work. The dedication of the temple is not described but presumably followed the pattern of Solomon's.[10] A number of things are noteworthy. This is a celebration by *the people of Israel*, the whole people of God, and as such looks back to the great celebration of Solomon's time and forward to the great multitude whom no one can count before the throne of God. This emphasis on continuity is an important part of the whole picture.

The words *celebrated* and *joy* are significant. This is no perfunctory and routine action. We are in the atmosphere of the Psalms and finding delight in God and his work. But this joy is not simply emotion, it is demonstrated in the sacrifices offered.[11] The twelve male goats emphasize again that a sin-offering was being made for all Israel (the procedure is described in Num. 7). The covenant is still valid and its provisions need to be kept.

c. The book of Moses (6:18)

This book is a fitting parallel to the preaching of Haggai and Zechariah. As already noticed, the prophets recall the people to the words of Moses and fundamental covenant loyalties. Here the word of God and its role in shaping the nation is again underlined. Some commentators have argued that there is inaccuracy here in that it was David not Moses who established *groups* and *divisions*.[12] However, Moses laid down the basic distinctions between priests and Levites while David refined them.[13] The authority of Moses lies behind all that is happening here. This also points to the coming of Ezra, *a scribe skilled in the Law of Moses, which the LORD, the God of Israel, had given* (7:4).

---

[9] Many of the commentators point out that 1 Esdras 7:5 states that it was the twenty-third day not the third. This may have been to suggest that the Passover followed immediately after the completion of the temple.

[10] 1 Kgs 8; 2 Chr. 7.

[11] Some commentators are rather churlish about this, comparing it unfavourably with the more lavish celebrations when Solomon dedicated the temple. But, in the spirit of Lev. 1, if they offered the equivalent of a dove or pigeon rather than a bull, they were giving all they could.

[12] E.g. Williamson (WBC), p. 84.

[13] See Num. 18; 1 Chr. 23 – 26.

3. Celebrating the Passover (6:19–22)

It is very fitting that this section of the book ends with a joyful celebration of the Passover which was at the heart of the nation's life and a continual reminder of the covenant mercies of God. Appropriately, too, the narrator reverts to Hebrew, after the Aramaic section relating to Darius.[14] Three matters are emphasized.

a. The return of regular patterns of worship

This would be in late April and was followed by the Feast of Unleavened Bread. We have here both a living link with that first passover of Exodus 12 as well as the sense of a joyful new start. There are also echoes of the accounts of the rededication of the temple during the great passovers of Hezekiah and of Josiah.[15] There is one difference, though. In 2 Chronicles 30:3 the priests are criticized for not consecrating themselves in sufficient numbers. Here the priests are mentioned first and with an emphasis on holiness. In the Chronicles' passages the Levites were responsible for slaughtering the passover lamb, although 2 Chronicles 30:17 makes it clear that this was done only when the father of a household was not pure. Here perhaps, the situation being a new one demanded that the Levites take a lead in re-establishing this great festival.

Unleavened Bread followed immediately.[16] Deuteronomy 16:3 speaks of 'the bread of affliction' which was a reminder of the hasty departure from Egypt. As we saw in chapter 1, this has been a new exodus and thus the emotion of joy is very prominent and the sense of gratitude to God pronounced. The return of regular patterns of worship, when it is truly fuelled not only by thanks for the past but open to what the living God is doing now, will truly anticipate the worship of heaven.

b. A welcome for the outsider

It is almost obligatory for some to sneer at the narrow exclusivism and nationalism of Ezra and Nehemiah. That view sits ill with 6:21. Two things only were required for participation in the Passover. The first was to separate from *the unclean practices of their Gentile neighbours.* Very probably in this context that particularly meant turning from the worship of pagan gods, as well as perhaps circumcision, which Exodus 12:44 and 48 particularly associate with admission to

---

[14] On the Aramaic sections in Ezra see also p. 76 and p. 108 note 2.
[15] 2 Chr. 30; 35.
[16] See Exod. 12:15–20; Lev. 23:6–8; Num. 28:17.

the Passover. Secondly, such people were to *seek* the Lord. The verb 'to seek' (*dāraš*) is a frequent one in the Old Testament and involves no mere cultic activity but a real engagement of heart, mind and will. Amos distinguishes false seeking (i.e. the idolatrous Bethel cult) from true seeking of God which is life itself.[17] Isaiah urges people to 'seek the Lord while he may be found' (55:6) and there it is a deep longing for the Lord's presence. Like the Thessalonians, it is a farewell to an old life and a joyful acceptance of a new one. Paul praises that young church who 'turned to God from idols to serve the living and true God, and to wait for his Son from heaven' (1 Thess. 1:9–10). This is no narrow clique. Kidner, as ever, puts it succinctly and memorably: 'The convert found an open door, as Rahab and Ruth had done.'[18]

c. A line drawn

Surprisingly the Lord is said to have brought this about by changing the attitude of *the king of Assyria* (v. 22). There is no evidence of a copyist's error so the explanation must be sought elsewhere. Some argue that in the Ancient Near East new dynasties and even new occupying powers were incorporated into existing king lists. Fensham[19] mentions a king list of Babylon which goes from the Assyrians to the Seleucids. However, the mention here is not part of a list and we need to look for another explanation.

Both Kidner[20] and Williamson[21] go in the right direction by pointing out that Assyria here is seen in the role of the traditional oppressor, as Babylon is to be in Revelation,[22] and they refer to Nehemiah 9:32 where the kings of Assyria are seen as the originators of the centuries of hardship. I want to explore this a little further and see how the mention here of the king of Assyria draws a line under the exile, which had originally been set in motion by the Assyrians.

We are accustomed to thinking of the exile as the destruction of Jerusalem and the temple and the deportation of the people to Babylon. That is not wrong, but when we read the account of that event in 2 Kings 25 we are struck by the laconic nature of the narrative and the lack of overt theological comment. In contrast, in 2 Kings 17 where the fall of Samaria is recorded with the deportation of the northern tribes to Assyria, we have a long section of theological

---

[17] Amos 5:4, 6.
[18] Kidner, p. 60.
[19] Fensham, p. 96.
[20] Kidner, p. 60.
[21] Williamson (WBC), p. 85.
[22] See e.g. 14:8; 18:2.

comment.[23] Significantly there Judah is specifically mentioned as also failing to obey the Torah,[24] and this section appears to do duty for the exile of both kingdoms. The author of Kings knows well that Judah's exile was delayed because of the great reformers Hezekiah and Josiah but also knows of the apostasy of Manasseh. It is interesting to see that the sins of 2 Kings 17:16–17 are those which were characteristic of Manasseh's reign.

Isaiah 10:5 speaks of Assyria as the rod of God's anger which will spell the end of the Northern kingdom. We know that the Assyrian was humbled when Hezekiah, unlike his father Ahaz, trusted the Lord;[25] but, sadly, having stood up to a bully, Hezekiah succumbed to flattery and surrendered to the blandishments of Babylon.[26] But the process by which the exile came was initiated by Assyria and now that process has ended.

Here the phrase *changed the attitude* recalls the earlier phrase *moved the heart* used of Cyrus in 1:1. This section ends with no doubt as to what lies behind history. Here we have a powerful illustration of Proverbs 21:1: 'The king's heart is in the hand of the LORD; he directs it like a watercourse wherever he pleases.'

Now the narrative is to jump almost sixty years to the coming of Ezra himself and we need to pause and review the journey we have travelled. Before looking at some of the characteristics of these early chapters of Ezra though, it would be worth having a glance at the decades between Ezra 6 and 7 in their wider context. By the end of chapter 6 we have reached 516 BC and Ezra's arrival at the beginning of chapter 7 is probably 458 BC.[27] We have already discussed 4:6–24 which tells of events in the reign of Xerxes (485–465 BC), but we probably have two other biblical witnesses to this period.

The book of Esther tells of events happening in the Persian city of Susa which had incalculable consequences for the entire nation. Had Haman succeeded, the entire nation, including the returned exiles, would have been obliterated. Surely we must see in this a satanic attempt to prevent the Messiah being born, as later through Herod he was to attempt to destroy him after birth. Esther illustrates vividly the universal nature of the God of Israel who is also the God of heaven. God has purposes of his grace for his people, even those who did not return to Jerusalem.

It is also possible that Malachi was active just before the return of Ezra to Jerusalem. If this is so we can glimpse more clearly the need

[23] 17:7–40.
[24] 17:19.
[25] 2 Kgs 18 – 19.
[26] 2 Kgs 20; Isa. 39.
[27] See Introduction pp. 17–20 for a discussion of the chronology involved.

for Ezra's preaching and Nehemiah's reforms as we read of mixed marriages, corrupt priesthood and financial irregularities. Every new generation needs the word given and applied, because reforming zeal soon runs out of steam. Malachi, the last prophetic voice before the Baptist proclaims the coming Messiah, calls the people back to Moses and speaks of the Elijah who is to come.[28] So, while Ezra is silent on this period, great events are happening and God is working out his purpose.

4. General comments on Ezra 1 – 6

We shall look at four complementary emphases which characterize these chapters and give them their particular flavour. It is in the blend of these, I suggest, that we can catch something of the fascination of this part of Scripture.

a. Providence and human responsibility

This is the fundamental theological principle underlying the book and the basic emphasis of which the other balancing truths I shall mention are, in a sense, particular examples. The providence of God is shown strikingly at the beginning when God 'stirred up the heart of Cyrus' (1:1, ESV) and at the end when again he *changes the attitude* of the king (6:22). This allows the human activities to proceed and eventually come to a conclusion with the rebuilt temple.

Providence is not visible in the way that human activity is. We see in chapter 2 the care and precision in the recording of those who returned, the first efforts at rebuilding, the twenty years of inactivity, the political scheming and the eventual success. Outwardly that is all that is happening. God's providence and his working behind the scenes, however, is embodied in the words of the prophets. At the beginning of the book, the words spoken through Jeremiah are the agents bringing about change (1:1). Haggai and Zechariah are raised up to renew flagging efforts (5:1–2; 6:14). Behind it all is the word of Moses (3:2; 6:18). The prophetic word is a powerful sign that God is at work.

b. Continuity and change

Since this is a work of God, these two aspects both mark it. God's unchanging purposes are worked out in ever-changing circumstances. Continuity is seen in a number of ways. This is not the

---

[28] Mal. 4:4–5.

building of a temple *de novo*, it is the rebuilding of Solomon's temple. The regulations for sacrifice are scrupulously carried out and the continuity with both Moses and David emphasized. The returning exiles in chapter 2 are closely linked with their forebears and their ancestral territories. All this emphasizes that what is happening is the re-establishment of Israel itself. This new exodus leads to a new settlement and the restoring of life and the regular institutions of worship. Moreover, the phrase *for all Israel* (6:17) takes us back beyond the immediate pre-exilic period to the time of Moses himself and the whole of the people of God.

But this situation is also a new one. There is no longer a Davidic king or indeed kingdom. This leads to prolonged negotiations with the Persian court as well as local officials. The new prophets apply the age-old message to the specific task in hand as well as pointing to a yet more glorious fulfilment. The great Psalm 136, sung at the laying of the temple's foundations (3:11), with its masterly survey of God in creation and history, comes with new meaning as once again 'the God of heaven' (Ps. 136:26) is praised at this fresh beginning.

c. Factual and evocative

Many things in these chapters do not instantly attract. Lists of names and extracts from official documents do not on first reading strangely warm our hearts. Yet, as we have seen, these passages root the events in the actual lives of real people and give an authenticity which is unmistakeable.

But there is far more to this than a mere chronicle of events. 'Here are events to learn from, not only to learn about.'[29] We have noticed the echoing of earlier Scriptures as we hear the music of the Psalms and see a new exodus, and hear the voices of contemporary prophets join with that of Moses and other messengers. We see this apparently local episode played out against the backdrop of the history of the mighty Persian Empire, but more than that as a significant moment in the eternal purposes of God.

d. Small canvas and big picture

The time from 538 to 516 BC covered by Ezra 1 – 6 is not long and does not seem to record very stirring events. Some have seen an excessive concern with ritual purity and lists of names. Indeed it is a small canvas and the events recorded do not appear to be very exciting.

[29] Kidner, p. 19.

But that is too narrow a view. Far more significant is its place in the big picture. The great biblical themes are here at this significant moment in the unfolding of God's purposes. We have here an important link in the chain which leads from the exile to the New Testament. We have the partial fulfilment of prophecies about the people of the Lord returning to Zion. Above all this is a story of the activity of God who has used pagan monarchs as well as prophets to carry out his purposes. The *house of God* in 1:3 and 6:22 forms an *inclusio* which gives the character to chapters 1 – 6, and in that time the house is built and the process of beginning again is underway.

The foundations have been laid both physically and spiritually and priorities have been established. *Israel* is back in the land and the worshipping life of the community has been restarted. Yet much remains to be done, and that is to occupy the next section of the book.

Ezra 7:1–10
8. God's man arrives

Those who have explored the byways of English literature may have come across *Tristram Shandy*,[1] a vast sprawling novel written by Lawrence Sterne in the eighteenth century. One of the most notable features of this novel is that the hero is not born until the third book. We may feel a similar sense of oddity here in Ezra 7, because only now more than halfway through the book appears the man after whom it is named. Some sixty years have passed since the events of chapters 5 and 6,[2] and some eighty since the early pioneers returned to Jerusalem to rebuild the temple.

Yet clearly the emphasis is on the divine timing – *after these things* (v. 1). *These things* are the completion and dedication of the temple and the celebration of the Passover (6:13–22), which had brought to completion the first stage of the return. 'After' is more than a marker of time; it is a reminder that celebration can be transitory and the re-establishment of Torah at the centre of the nation's life was essential if the purpose of the return from exile was to be fulfilled. Hence the emphasis here is on Ezra as being *a teacher well versed in the Law of Moses* (v. 6). Temple without Torah had proved disastrous before the exile,[3] so the next stage of the return is the establishing and teaching of the Law of Moses, and the man who is to do this now comes on to the stage.

1. A distinguished pedigree (7:1–5)

The length of this genealogy establishes the significance of Ezra, who is one of the Bible's great figures. The list of names gives the sense

---

[1] The full title is *The Life and Opinions of Tristram Shandy, Gentleman*, in nine volumes (London: Word, Dodsley, Beker and De Hondt, 1759–69).

[2] See Introduction p. 20 for a further discussion of the dating of Ezra and Nehemiah.

[3] See Jer. 7.

of God's providence over the generations preparing for Ezra and planning for the right moment when he would be most effective.[4] The most significant feature of the genealogy is the establishing of Ezra's priestly status deriving from his descent from Aaron. Yet the priests before the exile had often not been greatly helpful in maintaining Israel's spiritual life. When we think of figures such as Eli and his sons we see how low the institution could sink. Yet there are glimpses of better things. Jehoshaphat commissioned priests to teach the law,[5] and it is vital as the returned exiles settle down that the ancient order is restored (Malachi shows how this failed to happen). Yet Ezra is a figure who is to represent the best in the ancient order, and, as we now see, he is to be more.

2. A double gifting (7:6a)

Ezra is also a teacher. Not only is he connected to the line of Aaron, he calls the people back to the words of Moses, which are the words of God. He is a *scribe* (*sōper*), a word which in itself implies years of training and careful study. Not that this was always the case, for some treated their responsibilities lightly, and Jeremiah 8:8 speaks of 'the lying pen of the scribes' who tamper with God's law. This is to be in sharp contrast to the picture of Ezra here as a faithful and diligent teacher. He is further described as *well versed* (NIV); 'skilled' (ESV). The word *māhîr* has a variety of nuances: Psalm 45:1 uses it of a ready or prompt scribe and Proverbs 22:29 in a broader sense of someone who is skilful or diligent in their work. The implication here is something more than that Ezra was knowledgeable. Rather he had a clear and thorough grasp of the Torah and an ability to teach it and help others to understand.

It is also significant what is said of the Torah itself. Three affirmations are made. First, it is *of Moses*. Ezra's task was to teach the words of the great lawgiver, the foundational documents of the community. He is not seen as a compiler of traditions which may contain material which has a connection with Moses but have been overlaid and redacted in subsequent centuries. Nor is he simply a reviser; in Nehemiah 8 he is to be seen expounding that word which is not simply the authoritative record of the past but the living voice for the present.

Second, this is the covenant document; it is the word of Yahweh, God of Israel. This is a powerful underlining of the theme of continuity, which we noticed as a powerful presence in the first part of

---

[4] A longer list is provided in 1 Chr. 6:1–15 – both genealogies are selective.
[5] 2 Chr. 17:7–9.

the book. It is a reminder that the community had been formed at Sinai as the people gathered to hear the voice of the Lord.

Third, the Torah is *given*. This means that the law is not simply the opinions and reflections of Moses and those around him. The lawgiver has authority because he faithfully transmitted the Lord's words as they were given to him. Similarly what Ezra is to say will carry that authority as he faithfully in his day passes on that same message. Much of the contemporary dislike of the book of Ezra and Nehemiah stems from seeing them as late and inferior attempts to recreate a glorious past which was itself largely mythical.[6] It is difficult to get excited about events which never happened involving people who may or may not have existed.

3. A providential overruling (7:6b–7)

Here is a marvellous blend of God's providence and human responsibility. A similar phrase occurs in Nehemiah 2:8 which also shows powerfully both the unseen hand behind events and the necessary part of the human actors. The part of Artaxerxes in this is outlined more fully in the rest of the chapter, but as we saw already in relation to Cyrus in chapter 1, while the kings made their own decisions in accordance with their overall policies they were fulfilling the Lord's purposes.

What is also striking is the part Ezra played. The simple phrase *the king had granted him everything he asked* no doubt conceals anxious and tense times as Ezra pondered on the best way and time to approach the king and waited nervously for his answer. There is an important principle here. We must not let the great doctrine of providence turn us into passive pietists who say 'if we pray God will do all the work'. This is as misguided as the activists who imagine that the kingdom will only come if we are continually bustling around. Rather we must be ready to move when God opens the doors. This is where the earlier emphasis on Ezra as a scribe skilled in the Law of Moses comes together with the other aspect of his life as an official at the Persian court. God had been preparing him in both spheres for this task and thus when the door opened he was ready to go through it.

So we have no cloistered scholar nor a shallow activist; we have a man deeply schooled in the word of God who is also a man of planning and strategy. This is a good model for all of us who work for the kingdom of God. God's sovereign work, both in his overall

---

[6] This appears in an extreme form in L. L. Grabbe, *Ezra/Nehemiah* (London: Routledge, 1998), who dismisses Ezra as of virtually no historical significance.

strategy and in the microspheres of our lives, is a given, but we need to labour towards that end. This is powerfully expressed by Paul: 'To this end I labour, struggling with all his energy, which so powerfully works in me' (Col. 1:29). Thus when God is at work, his people are at work.

This is underlined in verse 7, which many see as a largely routine detail. Ezra did not come alone. A fuller account of those who returned will be given in chapter 8 but here we have a sample of those who came with him. They were a varied group, some of them prominent, others probably more behind the scenes. Gifted teachers like Ezra, strategic leaders like Nehemiah, are vital in the work for God, but no less vital are the rest of God's people. Building the kingdom of God is not a spectator sport and Paul in Ephesians 4 makes it very plain that all God's people have their work of ministry. All are important; hence the lists of names and the details of various kinds of work.

4. An auspicious arrival (7:8–9)

Here again there is that blend of routine detail with glimpses of the underlying significance of the events. We learn here the time involved in the journey, which would have taken some four months, between early April and early August. The journey would have been some 900 miles, much of it over fairly taxing territory and there must have been many hazards. The first day of the fifth month is more than a point of time, it has overtones of a new start.

However, there are a number of pointers to a much deeper significance in this journey. The names Babylon and Jerusalem are more than geography; they are pointers to the spiritual nature of this journey. The use of the verb 'go up' which is brought out in the ESV ('he began to go up from Babylonia') is an evidence that this is seen as a second exodus as well as echoing the journeys of pilgrims going up to the temple. Chapter 8 is to tell us of the fasting and praying which accompanied the beginning of the journey and of the natural fear and doubts about such a major undertaking as well as the sacrifices which marked its conclusion. This was a major stage in God's unfolding purposes.

But the decisive factor was that *the gracious hand of his God was on him*. The metaphor of God's 'hand' or 'arm' has its roots in the experience of God redeeming his people from Egypt. In Exodus there are many references to the outstretched arm of God and of Moses.[7] The work of God's hands also indicates God's power in

---

[7] Exod. 4:17; 6:1; 7:19; 13:3.

creation.[8] So the phrase here comes with all the associations of God as Creator of the world and Saviour of his people, who is again working decisively and effectively. This is the ultimate explanation of the significance of Ezra and the work in which he was involved. As we have seen, this whole project seemed low key and lacking in excitement and yet it was as much a work of God as more spectacular events, and it is a vital part of the overall story.

So it has always been in God's working with his people. There have been formidable enemies, stiff opposition and much discouragement in face of inadequate resources. God's counterattack has often seemed so feeble and inadequate. In the very early days when Eden had become Babel and the nations were in wholesale retreat from godliness, God's response was to set his hand on Abraham and amidst the raging and posturing of kings and empires to call him to another kind of city whose builder and architect was God. When the Roman emperor, the Herod family and the whole establishment were hostile or indifferent, God's response was a baby in an ox's stall. Thus did the Lord put down the mighty from their thrones. If our work, however insignificant it may seem, is undergirded by the gracious hand of the Lord, it will not only prosper but will last into eternity.

5. A good all-rounder (7:10)

Ezra was superbly qualified both by experience and activity to give a lead to this new phase of the work in Jerusalem and verse 10 sums up his gifts and endeavours. Here we have a fine and concise picture not simply of Ezra but a snapshot of a model reformer. We may compare this with the longer portrait of the teacher in Ecclesiastes 12:9–12 where there is a similar emphasis on the work and diligence of the one who studies and teaches. Here three activities of Ezra, all necessary and all done unstintedly, mark him out as God's man for this moment.

a. He was a student

He realized that he would be an effective teacher only insofar as he diligently studied his material. All effective teaching flows from the careful, painstaking and consistent study of our texts. In this case the Torah is read and grasped both in its broad sweep and in its detail. Not for Ezra a superficial glance and a glib stream of platitudes; he dug deeply in the treasures of the word and meditated on their significance.

[8] E.g. Isa. 19:25; 45:11; Pss 92:4; 138:8.

There is an important principle here for those who teach and preach the Scriptures. The key to effective preaching is first and foremost understanding how to handle the Bible in its different genres, emphases and its profound unity. Thus there is no shortcut to effective teaching; only unremitting and careful study. It is ironic that though there never has been a day when Bible study has been so accessible, with study Bibles, attractively produced notes and handbooks, not to mention the growing volume of audio-visual material, yet ignorance of the Bible is so profound. Such study will always be less glamorous than more instant ways of working but it will pay richly both in the life of the one who studies and in those who benefit from such studies.

b. He practised what he studied

Here he stands in the noble tradition of those who have not only heard and studied the word of God but have carried out its teachings. This was the foundation of the covenant community. Deuteronomy is full of exhortations to observe the Torah and to pass on these works to our children.[9] It was such observance that would keep Joshua in the true ways of the Lord.[10] It is failure to exemplify such obedience and observance which the prophets condemn.[11] Ezra was no mere theoretician; the study of the word no mere intellectual exercise.

It is always a danger that students of the word of God become interested in the intellectual aspects of that study in the same way as we might be interested in Bourbon France or astrophysics, without the study shaping our attitudes and behaviour. Sometimes in academia this can become an increasing concentration on the technical aspects of study without ever considering their implications. In many university departments biblical studies can become on the one hand an adjunct to ancient history and archaeology or on the other an aspect of philosophy or literary theory. Not that such study is wrong in itself, but for the Christian scholar it must be subordinated to the greater goals of godly living and godly teaching.

c. He was a teacher

This is the natural product of the other two. While study can easily become an end in itself, so study and observance which stop there can soon become sterile. Sometimes the right desire to guard the

[9] E.g. Deut. 5:32; 6:3; 8:1; 12:28; 16:12; 28:1; 32:46.
[10] Josh. 1:7–8.
[11] See especially Jeremiah: e.g. 3:13; 9:13; 17:23; 40:3; 42:21; 44:23.

purity of the gospel can become a negative retreat into a ghetto without the overwhelming desire to pass on the word. The way to guard the gospel is to pass it on. Thus in 2 Timothy Paul not only speaks of the God-breathed nature of Scripture[12] but urges Timothy to 'Preach the Word; . . . in season and out of season' (2 Tim. 4:2); having already urged him to pass on that word to other faithful teachers.[13] The disastrous result of failing to do this is seen at the end of Joshua. Moses had trained Joshua; Joshua had presumably trained the elders who outlived him.[14] Somewhere, however, these elders had failed to train the next generation and the result was the grotesque chaos of the book of Judges.

What Ezra taught was *decrees and laws* which is a shorthand for the totality of the Torah. The nuance of difference is that 'decrees' or 'statutes' (*ḥōq*) refer to divine decrees not only in relation to civil and ceremonial law but to the order God imposes on his creation.[15] 'Laws' or 'ordinances' translate *mišpāt* which are commands for the regulation of Israel's conduct. Together they show the divine and human aspects of the word of God: its givenness and authority and the necessity of translating the words into action. In Nehemiah 8 we are to have a glimpse of how Ezra, with others, taught the Torah in a ceremony at the Water Gate, and indeed if we look at the two books together that chapter is a fitting climax to them. Ezra is the wise teacher of the law who brings out of his storeroom new treasures as well as old.[16]

Ezra's place in the transmission of the Law of Moses was vital. As we know from the Gospels, not all his successors as scribes and teachers of the law followed his noble example. Nowhere is this more strikingly illustrated than in Matthew 23. Here Jesus both establishes the authority of the Torah: 'The teachers of the law and the Pharisees sit in Moses' seat. So you must obey then', but castigates the teachers: 'but do not do what they do, for they do not practise what they preach' (Matt. 23:2–3). In Ezra there is no divorce between teaching and living.

Derek Kidner has a characteristically lucid and insightful comment:

He is a model reformer in that what he taught he had first lived, and what he had lived he first made sure of in the Scriptures. With study, conduct and teaching put deliberately in this right order,

[12] 2 Tim. 3:16.

[13] 2 Tim. 2:2.

[14] Josh. 24:31.

[15] E.g. the waters (Job 26:10; 38:10) and the heavenly bodies (Job 38:33; Jer. 31:35–36).

[16] Matt. 13:52.

each of these was able to function properly at its best: study was saved from unreality, conduct from uncertainty, and teaching from insincerity and shallowness.[17]

These words are both a neat summation of the portrait of Ezra in these verses and a challenge to all who teach and preach the word of God.

[17] Kidner, p. 62.

Ezra 7:11–28
9. The king's heart is in the hand of the Lord

The words of Proverbs 21:1, which have been taken as the title for this chapter, provide a way into the exposition of this passage. Earlier passages in Proverbs have spoken of the authority of kings: their authoritative words; their anger; their capacity to open the way for others and their judgment.[1] But 21:1 shows the true source of all authority and the seat of all power. What Proverbs asserts is exemplified here in chapter 7. As the book moves into its second part we find the same providence at work that moved Cyrus in chapter 1. There we saw that Cyrus had his own reasons of policy for doing what he did, as Artaxerxes does here, but behind all that happens is *the hand of the Lord my God* (v. 9 echoed in v. 28).

Two very different sections comprise this passage and, at first glance, seem to sit awkwardly together. Yet if we focus on the interplay of God's providence and human responsibility we see that these are two sides of the same coin. The first section (vv. 11–26) is an official letter from Artaxerxes giving Ezra authority to carry out his task.[2] The second section (vv. 27–28) is a prayer of thanksgiving by Ezra himself.

1. The heart of the king (7:11–26)

Here we are in a world of officialdom, of permission granted, of detailed instructions and of state policy. Since this official document

---

[1] Prov. 16:10, 14; 20:2; 16:15; 20:8.
[2] This letter, like the other official documents earlier in the book (4:8 – 6:18), is written in Aramaic, the international language. From 7:27 the rest of the book is in Hebrew.

has been preserved for us in Scripture it clearly has significance beyond what may first appear.

a. The king's letter

The document begins with a reminder of both the political and religious situation (vv. 11–12). This is what in later times would be called a 'firman', a letter authorizing the bearer to carry out his duties in the king's name. Some have quibbled at the king's apparent knowledge of offerings and priests and Levites, but this document would almost certainly have been drafted, if not by Ezra, then by an official. The title 'king of kings' was particularly characteristic of Persian monarchs[3] and this is a further indication of the authenticity of the letter. Probably, therefore, *the priest, a teacher of the Law of the God of Heaven* is Ezra's official title. The phrase *the God of heaven* suggests another parallel with the edict of Cyrus (1:2).

This echo of Cyrus' policy continues in verse 13 with renewed permission for Israelites to return to Jerusalem. To the authority of the king is added that of his seven advisers (a similar group occurs in Esther 1:14). The phrase *the Law of your God, which is in your hand* confirms that what Ezra had was the Pentateuch (see comments on 7:6). This was to be the rule of life for the returned exiles.

To finance the project (vv. 15–20) we have both gifts from the royal treasury and freewill offerings both from native Babylonians and Babylonian Israelites. This reflected the Persian policy that magnanimity to different kinds of worship would be advantageous to the empire as a whole.[4] Details follow about the sacrifices and sacred vessels and assurances of further help from the royal treasury.

Instructions to provincial treasurers are given in verses 21–24. Some again have questioned the lavish amounts authorized but this must be seen in terms of Persian imperial policy. Judaea was on the fringe of the empire and its loyalty was important, thus Artaxerxes, again like Cyrus, was anxious to maintain good relations by ensuring the goodwill of the God of that particular people. This was not unique and can be paralleled from Egypt.[5]

Finally (vv. 25–26), Ezra was to establish that all those who were part of the Israelite community in the whole province 'Beyond the River' observed and lived by the Torah. This has also been seen as hopelessly idealistic, but see further the theological comments below.

[3] See Dan. 2:37.
[4] Two attempts to persuade Persian kings to act otherwise and suppress the faith of Israel ended disastrously for the perpetrators (Dan. 6 and Esther).
[5] Clines, p. 105. Cf. Williamson (WBC), pp. 104–105.

b. God's overruling

The reader may well feel 'so what?' at this point. This letter may well indeed be accurate and reflect the conditions of the time, but as a living word from God it appears to lack relevance. The first thing to remember is that this objection might have some force if this were simply a document unearthed by an archaeologist and of only historical interest. However, since it is sandwiched between the extended introduction to Ezra as teacher of the Law (vv. 1–10) and Ezra's doxology (vv. 27–28) there are plainly theological issues here and I want to comment on four of these.

The overruling of God to preserve his people has already been an important theme in the book but here it is particularly emphatic. That overruling is not simply in terms of the broad policy of the Persian kings, but in details such as the temple sacrifices, the amount of money and the official title of Ezra. This is an encouragement to trust God whose work is not simply of general benevolence but of detailed care. It is also a reminder of the importance on our part of giving attention to detail and avoiding the idea that what is slapdash is glorifying to God. This should not be dismissed as exaggerated detail. Many have seen the *hundred talents of silver* (v. 22) as hugely disproportionate. We should not hastily assume that we know exactly what the modern equivalents for ancient measures are, and thus we cannot assert that such a sum was impossible. The point is that the Lord to whom belong the gold and the silver will use the resources of creation to protect and preserve his people as and when he wills. In the same way, the gold, myrrh and frankincense brought by the Wise Men in Matthew 2, whatever their symbolic significance may have been, was probably used to finance the hurried trip to Egypt. The emphasis on *freewill offerings* (vv. 15–16) is particularly significant, recalling as it does Exodus 25:2 with its emphasis that offerings for the tabernacle are to be voluntary and the product of hearts which love God. As we have already seen, this is a new movement recalling the exodus and showing that the response to the overwhelming generosity of God is to be freewill offerings of hearts moved by his grace. Thus in the 'officialese' of this chapter we discern God's hand ensuring his people's safety and prosperity.

The overruling of God to preserve his word. Just as Cyrus did not imagine that his policy decisions were fulfilling the words of Jeremiah, so Artaxerxes cannot have known that his actions were helping to preserve the word of God for future generations. Doubtless he saw it as a policy of allowing subject nations to read their own writings and follow their own laws and customs. However, he is unwittingly giving legal sanction to the words of Moses: 'These commandments that I give you today are to be upon your hearts. Impress them on your children. Talk about them . . . ' (Deut. 6:6–7). It is ironic that what many of the kings of Judah and all the kings of Israel had failed to teach (and in many cases tried to suppress) is now being given official authorization by a pagan king. Surely verse 23 is a model statement of a true attitude to the word of God.

So it is that throughout the centuries God has preserved his word against all attacks and often used the most unexpected means to do so. For generations, until the recent past, the King James Version of the Bible was part of the fabric of our national life. Much of this was cultural, but who can say what the Spirit did in the lives of many who heard or read that word? We need to thank God more than we do for those who, often at great personal cost, translated the Scriptures and made them available. Names such as Wycliffe and Tyndale remind us of God's gift of his word.

The overruling of God to preserve the honour of his name. We can see this when we compare the phrase *the God of heaven* (vv. 12) with *their God in Jerusalem* (v. 16) and *the God of Jerusalem* (v. 19). We noticed in the exposition of chapter 1 that Cyrus was not a believer in Yahweh, but used the title 'of heaven' as one which the returning exiles would themselves use. To the Persian monarchs, Yahweh was simply the god whose province was Jerusalem. However, at the heart of Israel's faith was the conviction that Yahweh was no localized godlet – 'my help comes from Yahweh, the Maker of heaven and earth' (Ps. 121:2). Thus, in a document designed by Artaxerxes to demonstrate his multi-faith credentials and tolerant policies, the Holy Spirit shows us the real state of affairs. This, too, at a time when Israel's religion was seen as one of the many in the world supermarket rather than a declaration that Yahweh is king and that the nations will be judged by him. From this follows the fourth theological comment.

The overruling of God which points to the future. Some commentators deny that this passage has an eschatological thrust.[6] However, verse 25 especially, speaking of a community dominated by the Torah, points to the final kingdom when, according to Isaiah 2 and Micah 4, 'the law will go out from Zion, the word of the LORD from Jerusalem' (Isa. 2:3; Mic. 4:4). In a similar vein, Malachi speaks of the pure offerings 'because my name will be great among the nations, says the LORD Almighty' (Mal. 1:11). This eschatological perspective is necessary because, without denying its actual relevance to Ezra's own time, it shows that time as part of a wider movement which will culminate in the honouring of the Lord's name

---

[6] E.g. Williamson (WBC): 'Eschatological hopes are, of course, another matter, but there is no evidence of their inclusion here', p. 104.

by the whole earth. The details remain obscure but the outcome is certain.

> I cannot tell how he will win the nations,
> how he will claim his earthly heritage,
> how satisfy the needs and aspirations
> of east and west, of sinner and of sage.
> But this I know, all flesh shall see his glory,
> and he shall reap the harvest he has sown,
> and some glad day his sun will shine in splendour,
> when he the Saviour, Saviour of the world, is known.[7]

Thus, behind the heart of king Artaxerxes and the advice of his counsellors lies the hand of the Lord, and to that we now turn.

2. The hand of the Lord (7:27–28)

The tone now changes and we move from the official to the personal, from implicit theology to rousing doxology. This personal note is to continue until the end of chapter 9. Breaking into song is a feature of biblical faith and a reminder to us that our theology always must end in worship. On a grand scale there is Moses' great song in Exodus 15; on a smaller scale Ezekiel's exclamation: 'May the glory of the LORD be praised in his dwelling place!' (Ezek. 3:12). There are the great songs in Luke 1 and 2 which herald the coming of the Saviour and the great 'Hymn to Christ' in Philippians 2:6–11. Many other examples demonstrate that a living faith continually turns to poetry for its full expression. Moreover song is a fitting response to a divine salvation to which we have made no contribution. All there is left to us is to praise. Yet there is much theology as well as the overflow of emotion in this doxology of Ezra. The sense of the overruling providence of God is expressed in *the hand of the LORD* and Ezra's response in *I took courage*. Ezra strikes three notes in this little hymn of praise.

a. Thanksgiving for the past

God is now called *the God of our fathers* because what is happening here is a renewal of the promises to the patriarchs of land and prosperity which the exile had apparently disrupted. Here the emphasis on the temple is underlined: *to bring honour to the house of the LORD*

---

[7] William T. Fullerton (1857–1932), hymn: 'I cannot tell why he whom angels worship'.

(NIV); 'to beautify the house of the LORD' (ESV). Is Ezra perhaps reflecting on the words of Isaiah 60:7: 'I will beautify my beautiful house' (ESV); NIV, more idiomatically, but less accurately, 'I will adorn my glorious temple'? God is faithful, and as we have seen, has moved the king's heart to bring about the rebuilding of his house; *God of our fathers* encapsulates the faithfulness of the Lord to his people.

b. Confidence in the present

The remembering of God's past faithfulness brings confidence and courage to take action in the present. Ezra is not one who bewails past glories and allows nostalgia to blind him to present needs and opportunities. We are reminded of the intimidating experience of approaching the king and his *powerful officials*. This experience was to be one which Nehemiah shared[8] and only because of the *hand of the LORD* would either man be successful. This is why providence is no abstract doctrine but a major cause for praise and a strong bulwark for faith. The Lord is not trapped in the past but still working out his purposes and a rewarder of those who come to him in faith.

c. Looking to the future

Ezra realizes that he must not simply give thanks for the past and show confidence in the present but make plans for the future. The next chapters are to show us how fraught with difficulty that was to be. Yet this is the pattern of the life of faith, which always has to look beyond the seen problems to the unseen God. Ezra here shows the true realism of faith. There is no foolish super-spirituality, which tries to deny the role of the king and his officials. Nor is there a cringing before them, which suggests that their power is absolute. He knows very well the strength and danger posed by the Persian Empire but he knows that the God who made heaven and earth and who brought his people out of Egypt is far greater than his enemies and will use them to carry out his purposes.

At the heart of Ezra's faith and praise is the God of the covenant whose steadfast love endures for ever. Indeed the word NIV translates as *good favour* (v. 28) is the great covenant word *ḥesed*, often translated 'steadfast love'. That covenant had endured the fires of exile and would remain in all the changing circumstances of the future.

---

[8] Neh. 2:1–5.

The theme of Ezra's prayer is well expressed in the following hymn:

> How good is the God we adore!
>   Our faithful unchangeable Friend:
> His love is as great as His power,
>   And knows neither measure nor end!
>
> 'Tis Jesus, the First and the Last,
>   Whose Spirit shall guide us safe home:
> We'll praise Him for all that is past,
>   And trust Him for all that's to come.[9]

---

[9] Joseph Hart (1712–68), hymn: 'How good is the God we adore'.

Ezra 8:1–36
10. Another exodus

As the story continues we are once again reminded of the interplay of God's providence and human activity. The *hand of our God* is again mentioned (v. 22), but the human response, sometimes a most inadequate one, is also prominent. For many who returned now there can have been little incentive other than a dawning conviction that this was right for them and that the time had come to return to Jerusalem. In the event, a sizeable party of some 5,000 were assembled and undertook the journey. We shall look at the chapter as it unfolds in five stages.

1. More than a list of names (8:1–14)

Ezra never allows us to forget that there are real people involved here at every stage (as we have already seen in ch. 2) and that each, named and unnamed, was a living person who took this risk. It is indeed, as Kidner says, 'a forbidding list of names and numbers',[1] but there are significant implications here which go beyond the immediate and occasional. Formally the list falls into three parts: priests (v. 2a); noble families (vv. 2b–3a); lay or ordinary families (vv. 3b–14). *Phinehas* and *Ithamar* suggest a connection with Aaron.[2] *Hattush* is mentioned in 1 Chronicles 3:22 as a member of the royal line. Many of the names in verses 3b–14 can be found in Nehemiah 3. However, a number of significant points arise.

The first is that many of those returning are descendants of those who had been part of that first generation who had come to Jerusalem nearly eighty years before. We have no way of telling how conscientious these families had been in carrying out Moses' command

[1] Kidner, p. 65.
[2] Exod. 6:23–25.

to teach their children,[3] but plainly some at least must have caught Ezra's vision and this would hardly have happened if, to mix the metaphor, the soil had not already been prepared. This is both an encouragement to keep on training each new generation even when the fruits are not obvious, and also a warning, especially for heads of families, both the human and Christian families, not to neglect the vital task on passing on the gospel to our children and grandchildren. Joshua 24:31 speaks of how the people of Israel in that day remained faithful to the Lord 'through the lifetime of Joshua and of the elders who outlived him'. However, by Judges 2:11–13 they had turned to Baal and the Ashteroths. Clearly the elders who outlived Joshua had failed to teach as they themselves had been taught. Paul similarly urges Timothy to entrust the gospel to faithful witnesses (2 Tim. 2:2). Each new generation needs to hear afresh the life-changing word.

It has been pointed out[4] that it was twelve lay families who returned. This is significant. Ezra and other post-exilic books are anxious to see this remnant as the true heirs to the promises and the true inheritors of the privileges of the twelve tribes. The remnant are carrying the whole weight of God's purposes and ultimately to them and from them is to come the Messiah.

2. Where are the Levites? (8:15–20)

The assembled company now pause for three days at the river or *canal that flows towards Ahava*.[5] Ezra used that time to good effect, because, on checking that all was well, he discovered that there were no Levites. Their reluctance to return with the early pioneers has already been noted in 2:40 and shows again the drastic nature of this commitment to which they were being called. It is likely that the Levites had not responded to the call because of the chance to own property and settle in Babylon had proved much more attractive than the strict routines of temple service. Ezra's concern for Levites is related to his concern of passing on the faith through the generations. While there would be functioning Levites, there needed to be new people continually taking their places and providing continuity of leadership.

Ezra's method of dealing with this shows his wisdom and effectiveness as a leader. The first nine (v. 16) he called together *were*

[3] Deut. 6.
[4] See e.g. Williamson (WBC), p. 111.
[5] Ahava is otherwise unknown. The river cannot be the Euphrates but may have been one of the canals which had been constructed as part of the defensive system of Babylon.

leaders which presumably means people of proven standing and competence; the other two were *men of learning* who presumably provided scribal and other expertise. The fact that Casiphia, where they were sent, is twice called 'the place' (see ESV) probably implies that a sanctuary was there. The name is otherwise unknown. The fact that Ezra *told them what to say* (v. 17) shows the importance he attached to the choosing of Levites.

The leading figure among the Levites who answered the call was Sherebiah. He turns up several times in the story (again in verse 24 and then in Neh. 8:7; 9:4–5). His particular family was that of Mahli, son of Merari and grandson of Levi.[6] This was the family traditionally associated with the carrying of the tabernacle.[7] In the event, thirty-eight Levites answered the call. This is a small number and again reflects the lack of enthusiasm among the Levites generally.[8]

Whatever the difficulties, however few may have responded, Ezra is in no doubt that the *gracious hand of God* is directing the whole enterprise (v. 18). On the human level there would be the long process of trying to persuade people to come and disappointment when many would not. Yet behind the scenes God's gracious purposes were at work calling people to do his will and preparing them for the task. Ezra is continually calling us to look beyond the mundane and routine and see the hand of God working out his purpose as year succeeds to year.

3. Calling on God (8:21–23)

Before turning to further practical steps, Ezra turns to the Lord and places the whole matter in his hand. Fasting is a clearing of the decks for action and touching base to concentrate on fundamental realities. The fast is not an end in itself but an opportunity for the people to humble themselves before God and ask for his protection on the coming journey. Both the fasting and the humbling were a demonstration of their total dependence on God. There is realism here, particularly shown by the reference to children and possessions, both of which made them especially vulnerable. They had done all the preparations, they had the king's authorization and yet they were very exposed.

Two matters particularly call for comment. The first is the phrase in verse 21 which the NIV renders *a safe journey*. This is more literally 'a straight way', the phrase which Isaiah 40:3 uses of

[6] Exod. 6:16–19.
[7] Num. 3:33–37; 4:29–33.
[8] See ch. 2, particularly 2:43–58, for further comments on the temple servants.

preparing the way of the Lord. Here again the new exodus motif is being suggested and thus the Lord's endorsement of the enterprise.

The second is Ezra's honesty about not asking the king for an escort and his not doing so as an act of faith. We must not take this as an absolute principle. Rather it was his conviction that, for him, on that occasion, this would have been a lack of faith. Nehemiah, however, was to accept such an escort and see it as part of God's provision. Once again Kidner sums the matter up shrewdly: 'Both were attitudes of faith, and each in its different way (like the options in Rom. 14:6) gave acceptable honour to God.'[9]

The source of Ezra's faith is again in *the gracious hand of our God* (v. 22), and we can sense his grateful relief in verse 23: *he answered our prayer.*

The stories of the life of faith in Scripture are not there as blueprints of how we are to behave. Rather they show us people of faith wrestling with the same kind of issues as us and not finding them easy and straightforward. This is not contrasting Ezra's more 'spiritual' approach with Nehemiah's more 'practical' one. Both men looked at the situation and took, after prayer and reflection, the course which seemed right for the time. After all, both trusted in God; an armed escort was a precaution not a guarantee of safety.

4. The journey and the arrival (8:24–30)

Here again Ezra acts in the spirit of Moses as he gives twelve priests and twelve Levites responsibility for the transporting of the treasure, which is in line with the regulations in Numbers 3 and 4. He takes personal responsibility: *I weighed out . . .* (vv. 25, 26). The list is orderly: silver and gold itself followed by silver and gold vessels. Such valuable objects were a great responsibility as well as representing a considerable risk.

That this was no mere manual labour is emphasized in verses 28–30. They were *consecrated* as well as the artefacts themselves. Thus any temptation to steal or misuse would be powerfully guarded against. *The house of our God in Jerusalem* (v. 30) is a reminder of the purpose of this whole expedition. The holiness of God is to be a powerful theme in the next two chapters and both people and objects dedicated to him must partake of that holiness. Thus this little section is full of that deeper significance we have so often seen in the story so far.

[9] Kidner, p. 66.

5. Coming home (8:31–36)

This journey, of approximately 900 miles, is passed over with little comment because what mattered was the destination.[10] Yet there are two hints in verse 31 which point to its deeper significance. The word 'departed' (ESV) is literally 'pulled up their tent pegs', and is thus one of the many comparisons with the desert journeyings of the Israelites. Also the word 'delivered' (ESV) is more emphatic than *protected* (NIV) and the power of God the Saviour is again emphasized. This need not necessarily mean that there were many visible dangers from which they were rescued but rather that the protection of God ensured that no such incidents occurred.

Two kinds of activities mark their return. The first is the handing over of the precious objects which had arrived safely. Again there is the concern for detail and careful organization which has been a feature of the narrative. Verse 34 underlines the scrupulous and meticulous attention given to ensure that all was in order.

But since these vessels were not effective in themselves, but rather aids to the true worship of God, verse 35 outlines the sacrifices offered to the Lord, as verse 36 records the fulfilling of obligations to humans. The account shifts to the third person and this may indicate an editorial note to round off the whole section. In the burnt offering the entire animal was burned and this symbolized total consecration to the Lord.[11] This, more than speculation about multiples of seven or twelve, is the probable emphasis here. The whole story had been one of God's faithfulness and the response to that, which involved the consecration of all concerned. The project is rounded off when the obligations to humans are also discharged (v. 36). We are, however, left in no doubt where the centre of gravity lies: this was for the house of God and the object was to re-establish the true worship of God in the midst of his people.

As we review this chapter, three matters are central. The first is the communal nature of what was happening. Ezra could not carry out this task on his own; people were needed to do menial work such as carrying vessels and weighing out gold and silver articles. This was a truly communal effort, with the members of the body playing their part. Such passages often occur in the Bible and show the concern of the true leader for those who had been a vital part of the work. We can cite, for example, 2 Samuel 23:8–39 where not only the exploits of the great champions are recorded, but otherwise

[10] We may compare Matt. 2 where the journey of the Wise Men is passed over without comment, all the attention being on their arrival and their worship of the King.

[11] Lev. 1.

unknown men are honoured. A similar passage is Romans 16:1–15 where Paul names with affection those who had stood with him. Such recognition of others is surely one of the signs of a true leader and points finally to the day when the Lord, the righteous judge, will honour all those who love his appearing.

The second is the emphasis on the *hand of God* (vv. 18, 22, 31). This both underlines the theological weight and the practical reality of the phrase. In verse 22 it is a statement about God in salvation and judgment and a general theological comment on the overruling of all that happens and the accountability of everyone to the Lord. In verses 18 and 31 this general providence is more specifically applied to the events of the beginning and end of the journey. Great doctrines both expand the mind, lead to praise and work out in the everyday realities of life.

The third matter is a reminder that the purpose of this journey is to build up *the house of our God* (vv. 17, 30, 33, 36). This has been the great theme of the book and has underlined the fact that everything is being done for one purpose alone and that is to ensure the presence of the Lord among his people. The frequent allusions to the exodus have been noted. The emphasis on *the LORD, the God of your fathers* (v. 28) and *sacrificed burnt offerings to the God of Israel* (v. 35) underline this connection and especially the reason why the tabernacle was first made: 'have them make a sanctuary for me, and I will dwell among them' (Exod. 25:8). All of this shows that Ezra's mission was part of a work of God among his people and was to be a significant moment in their ongoing history.

Ezra 9:1–15
11. Faithless people; faithful God

> If you can meet with Triumph and Disaster
> and treat those two impostors just the same.[1]

Thus wrote Kipling, and here Ezra, having experienced modest triumph in the safe journey and arrival in Jerusalem, now faces a major disaster.[2] When Kipling describes these two circumstances as 'impostors' he is not meaning that they do not happen, rather that these are a background to life, not its main reality. Ezra had little time to be contented, much less euphoric, when he was confronted with a problem that struck at the heart of what this community was about.

Chapters 9 and 10 together form the final section of the book of Ezra and are a blend of narrative, prayer and the last of the lists. The tone is sombre and the sense of urgency is great. The contrast between what might have been expected and what actually happened is underlined by the opening phrase of 9:1: *After these things had been done*, probably referring to the events of 8:1 which, as we have seen, were a dawning of hope and a sense that the community was being organized and energized in a godly way. We shall look at chapter 9 under two broad divisions: the faithlessness of the community and the faithfulness of God.

1. The faithlessness of the community (9:1–5)

It is not entirely clear who *the leaders* (v. 1) were, especially since in verse 2 they appear to include at least some of their number in the

[1] Rudyard Kipling, poem: 'If', 1910.
[2] The timing of chapter 9 is related to the dating of Ezra and Nehemiah. Some want to place Ezra's reading of the law (Neh. 8) between chapters 8 and 9 of Ezra. See further the Introduction pp. 17–20.

sin they report. Williamson[3] suggests that they may have been district governors (such as those mentioned in Neh. 3:6–12). In any case they recognized the need for action and took it. A number of issues need to be addressed.

a. What was at stake?

The report of the leaders concerns *detestable practices* (v. 1) which here is seen as intermarriage with the non-Israelite population. Unfavourable comparisons have been drawn between the open and welcoming atmosphere of Ruth and the exclusiveness and rigidity of Ezra. But this is a superficial view, however much it may ring bells with contemporary dislike of anything which can be called discrimination.

The first point to notice is that marriage with foreigners was never forbidden in itself. Apart from Ruth, there are illustrious examples of such marriages such as Joseph and Moses himself.[4] Behind this is the welcome given to foreigners to become part of the covenant community, flowing from the promise to Abraham that through him and his descendants all the families of the earth would be blessed.[5] This is illustrated in Genesis 17 where circumcision is not only for Abraham's family but for the foreigners in his household. When Israel leaves Egypt 'many other people went up with them' (Exod. 12:38). Clearly the motive here is not racial prejudice or narrow nationalism; something deeper is at stake and to that we now turn.

b. Breaking the covenant

So far in Ezra (not least in ch. 8), we have seen the deliberate echoes of the exodus and now Ezra himself is in many ways playing the role of Moses. In chapter 3 we saw how the early pioneers were concerned to follow precisely the regulations laid down by God through Moses for the offering of sacrifices. Now here there is another deliberate echo of the Pentateuch as Ezra endeavours to establish godliness at the centre of the community.

This is shown first of all by linking the *neighbouring peoples* with names which echo the early inhabitants of the land when the Israelites first entered it. Exodus 34:11–16 and Deuteronomy 7:1–6 particularly mention these nations as being a snare, tempting people to idolatry. Indeed the history of the nation after the conquest bears sad and eloquent witness to that. There are few more chilling chapters

[3] Williamson (WBC), p. 130.
[4] Gen. 41:45; Num. 12:1.
[5] Gen. 12:3.

in the Bible than 1 Kings 11 where the springtime freshness of Solomon's early reign and the 'high Midsummer pomps'[6] of his middle years become the blasted winter of his old age, and the historian notes 'As Solomon grew old, his wives turned his heart after other gods, and his heart was not fully devoted to the LORD his God' (1 Kgs 11:4). Ezra realizes that this is no little local difficulty but something which strikes at the heart of the returned community. Israel is again lapsing into the very activities which led to the exile in the first place.

The neighbouring peoples may not be identical with those earlier groups ethnically, but spiritually and morally they represent an identical danger. The earlier words remain valid and the danger to *the holy race* (v. 2) remains real. The phrase used is literally 'holy seed' which is a striking reminder of the danger not only to the nation as a whole, but the believing remnant which is so described in Isaiah 6:13. Malachi 2:15 uses the phrase again in connection with unfaithfulness to the covenant. As was often the case before the exile, the failure was the greater in that leaders were heavily implicated.[7]

It is probable that what happens here is an indication that Ezra's calling people back to faithfulness to the Scriptures was already having an impact. Such exposure to the word of God will always reveal sin and call people to repentance. Ezra was challenging the 'holy seed' with the foundation documents of God's ancient covenant and showing its abiding relevance to that day. Surely this conviction that the Bible speaks today is what lies behind the series of which this exposition is a part. In our days of lax behaviour and disdain for God's creation order in marriage, we need to listen well to what Ezra says.

So often our problem in the contemporary church and our embarrassment at passages like this is that we have lost a true sense of the holiness of God and thus a true awareness of our own sin. The baleful results of such a cavalier attitude to God is seen in Malachi, with worthless 'sacrifices' and a total failure of the priests to teach the word of God. The word which sums it all up is *unfaithfulness* (v. 4) – a refusal to treat God seriously. Behind the marriage failures lay a more profound failure: a breakdown of the covenant relationship with the Lord.

Because of our own indifference to sin, and, in some cases, British stiff upper lip, we may well find Ezra's reaction in verses 3 and 5 embarrassing rather than humbling. Yet such symbolic actions are not mere gestures, they show profound concern for the honour of

---

[6] Matthew Arnold, poem: 'Thyrsis', 1865.
[7] See ch. 12 pp. 134–137.

God. Moreover these are representative acts, with Ezra acting on behalf of the whole people. Tearing of clothes was often symbolic of grief at someone's death.[8] Ezra wanted to shatter the peoples' complacency and apathy and dramatic actions were a way of doing this.

Verse 4 is another indication that already his teaching of the Torah was having an effect – *everyone who trembled at the words of the God of Israel* recalls the words of Isaiah spoken some two hundred years earlier: 'This is the one I esteem: he who is humble and contrite in spirit, and trembles at my word' (Isa. 66:2). Ezra had probably sat down in some public place where people could see him. Although he was not personally guilty, Ezra is identifying with the people in their sinfulness and, again like Moses, acting as an intercessor on their behalf.

Verses 5 and 6 show that Ezra did not rush into prayer but prepared himself by inward meditation as well as outward action for what he was to say to the Lord. The particular posture Ezra adopts for prayer is not given as a necessary model to follow but rather indicates his humility – *fell on my knees* – and his total reliance on God – *my hands spread out to the LORD my God*. His preparation for prayer anticipates the prayer itself in that it does not too readily rush to a happy ending with a cavalier attitude of taking God's grace for granted. Too often we presume on God's instant favour and thus regard behaviour such as Ezra's as fanatical.

2. The faithfulness of God (9:6–15)

Here we have one of the Bible's great prayers. Some general comments first and then we shall examine it in more detail. The prayer it most resembles is Daniel 9:4–19 and we will look at parallels as we proceed. The striking feature here is that the prayer is almost entirely confession with no real petition because Ezra is so conscious of sinfulness.

The prayer is both clearly structured and heartfelt. There is no contradiction between these. Plainly this is the prayer that Ezra spoke on that occasion, but as the book is put together, the words here are carefully written down to express in writing its impact for future generations. Different people will have preferences for set or spontaneous prayers. However, we need not deprive ourselves of either. The value of set and structured prayers is their support in times of spiritual dryness. For nearly fourteen years, although I come from a very different tradition, I found the discipline of set daily prayers in an Anglican theological college an important element

[8] E.g. Jacob in Gen. 37:34 and David in 2 Sam. 1:11.

in my own spiritual life. Yet there is also an important place for spontaneous prayers and for various combinations of both. Here we shall find Ezra using the words of Scripture which speak to the moment and situation he is in and which provide a blend of the traditional and the spontaneous.

The prayer flows from and is directed to Ezra's particular situation. Yet it goes far beyond as it links the present crisis with those in the past and looks to the future. While the particular issue is that of marriage, the reference to *detestable practices* (v. 11) shows that this is simply a specific example of unfaithfulness. Indeed it is the whole issue of disobedience to God which is at stake – *shall we again break your commands?* (v. 14) – and the whole doctrine of the remnant.[9] Thus the prayer has direct relevance to us and it challenges our frequent disregard for God's word.

The time of the prayer is significant: *at the evening sacrifice* (v. 5). This is the time in Daniel 9:21 when Gabriel is sent to Daniel in answer to his prayer. The remarkable thing in the Daniel passage is that the temple has yet to be rebuilt and for seventy years no sacrifices had been offered. Yet the realities behind these sacrifices remained and they pointed to the 'once for all' sacrifice which was to fulfil and supersede them and to be the complete forgiveness for the sins mourned so deeply both by Daniel and Ezra. Here Ezra must have wondered if the restoration of the sacrifices and the rebuilding of the temple had been abortive. Yet the sacrifice to which this 'evening sacrifice' pointed was both necessary because of the sins confessed here and the full answer to them.

We shall examine the prayer itself in five sections.

a. The sin which God judges (9:6–7)

Ezra begins by identifying with the people's sin: *I am too ashamed and disgraced* (v. 6). The singular quickly changes into plural as he acts as spokesman and confessor for the people. Both individual and corporate responsibility matter. Sin needs to be repented of individually. So often general and corporate confessions can be ignored as we imagine we are not personally guilty. Yet sin is also corporate; by our individual sinfulness we contribute to the community's sin. This is true historically as well. We cannot escape the effect of the sins of earlier generations nor the consequences of our sins for future generations.

Ezra uses two powerful metaphors: sins *higher than our heads* and guilt which reaches *to the heavens*. It is as if the accumulated

---

[9] See the exposition of Ezra 1.

sins of generations had become visible obstacles which threatened judgment and despair and had hidden the face of God. This sin had resulted in exile (both Northern and Southern kingdoms) and thus their history had itself been a punishment. Ezra here shows he understood clearly that the exile was no historical accident but brought about by God as a punishment for sin.

But Ezra's words here show more than a horror for sin, they show a true sense of the holiness of God. The reason he feels so disgraced and ashamed is because of the God he worships who cannot look on and tolerate sin. The mention of *kings* and *priests* (v. 7) is a reminder of the guilt of the leaders of the people who were primarily responsible. This is something which Isaiah had particularly condemned two centuries before.[10] Like Isaiah, Ezra here trembles before the Holy One of Israel. Ezra's God was not one whose 'job' it was to forgive sin[11] but someone who could not overlook it and had to punish it. So here there is no call for mercy, simply a stark confession of failure.

b. The grace which God gives (9:8–9)

Since this is not 'cheap grace' and the sin has been fully acknowledged, Ezra can now turn to God's grace which can cover all our sin. The *remnant* is an idea which we have come across already and which is the guarantee of the eventual fulfilment of God's purposes, for one day the Messiah will come from and to that remnant who wait 'for the consolation of Israel' (Luke 2:25). The *brief moment* is the period of some eighty years since the first group returned and whose activities had been overruled by the gracious providence of God. Further, the word *remnant* has a negative implication in the sense of the small number, but also a positive one in the sense that God had preserved them and would continue to do so. The word NIV translates as *firm place* is literally a 'tent peg' and is used in Isaiah 54:2 of the restored Zion. Here the reference is to God's renewed presence in the midst of his people, which results in *light to our eyes* because of the sense that the Lord is still at work. Politically they are not free; they are still under the rule of the Persian kings but yet the return to the land was part of God's continuing purposes for them.

We are reminded again of the purpose of their return from exile: *to rebuild the house of our God*. The sheer vulnerability of that project (seen already in earlier chapters of Ezra) is shown not to be

---

[10] See particularly Isa. 1.

[11] The reference is to the aphorism, 'The good God will forgive me; that's his job', variously attributed to the Empress Catherine of Russia and the philosopher Heine.

the most significant feature of it. Rather the reality is the protection of God. The *wall of protection* is a powerful metaphor of God's care for them. This is a similar idea to Zechariah 2:5, where the Lord, speaking of Jerusalem, says, 'I myself will be a wall of fire around it . . . and I will be its glory within'. Once again the building of the temple and the hardships of the return are seen in the widest context as a powerful manifestation of the presence of the living God. Williamson points out that the term can be used to mean a wall round a vineyard;[12] this would give a further nuance of the vine brought from Egypt and planted in the promised land[13] and underline the continuity of God's purpose.

The grace of God is the experience of God's faithfulness and tenderness which the community had experienced regularly, and which even after the exile still shines brightly and still gives hope. But Ezra is so distressed with the present situation that he now turns again to the faithlessness of the people, made worse by the continual giving of the word of God.

c. The word which God sends (9:10–12)

The indictment of the people is now expressed in the words of Scripture. They have not sinned unwittingly but have been faithless and disobedient to the word God has sent through the prophets. Here, Ezra uses similar language to Daniel 9; see, for example, verse 11 of that chapter: 'The curses and sworn judgments written in the Law of Moses, the servant of God, have been poured out on us, because we have sinned against you.' The authority of Moses, as archetypal prophet, is underlined here in the allusions to Leviticus and Deuteronomy. In Ezra, as in Daniel, the echoes of various passages of Scripture show the conviction that in Scripture following Moses, as well as in the words of the great lawgiver himself, God is speaking. Scripture is speaking into every situation and concerned not only with the facts but with the inner meaning of those facts.

The basic passages about polluted land are in Leviticus 18:25–30 and 20:22–24 in the Holiness Code and in Deuteronomy 7:1–6, which also contains references to the surrounding nations. 2 Kings 21:10–11 has a similar passage about the dreadful reign of Manasseh and the prophetic rebukes. Passages such as Isaiah 1:19–20 and Jeremiah 7:25–26 show both the authoritative teaching of the prophets and the persistence of the problem, which is also seen in Malachi 2:10–16. The injunction to turn away from impurity is

12 Williamson (WBC), p. 136.
13 Ps. 80:8–11.

underwritten by a repetition of the ancient promise of enjoying the land and the future perspective: *leave it to your children as an everlasting inheritance* (v. 12). The old practices were recurring and heeding the Scriptures was the only way to put these right. The grace of God was no excuse to disobey the commands of God, and Ezra is very afraid that a new disaster will come.

d. The fear which God inspires (9:13–14)

Ezra is aware that God had not punished the nation as they deserved. They had been exiled but not completely wiped out and the Lord had graciously allowed them to return. Again, echoing Exodus 32:10, he can envisage the destruction of the whole community. Just as then, God could have made a nation from others.[14] The grace of God, which Ezra has celebrated, does not remove or minimize the fear of God. Indeed it is only when we fear God that we can appreciate his grace. Thus the psalmist says: 'But with you there is forgiveness; therefore you are feared' (Ps. 130:4). If we do not tremble before God we shall see his love simply as rather weak benevolence, our faith will lack depth and an anaemic complacency will replace a robust sense of his presence.

e. The praise which God deserves (9:15)

Ezra concludes his prayer with what is in effect praise of God the righteous one and a reiteration of the community's unworthiness. The righteousness of God is at the heart of all true praise because it is both a reminder of his goodness as well as his greatness and a salutary underlining that he is in heaven and we are on earth. Even if God's righteousness leads to the punishment of his people he is still to be praised, and Ezra does not dilute this by asking for mercy. Rather, with Abraham he believes that the Judge of all the earth will do right.[15]

This chapter has contained little for our comfort or our desire, and as we leave it, three observations can be made. The first is that sin is insidious and affects the whole community, not simply the direct participants. These are not isolated acts which affect a few individuals and families and leave others untouched. The situation here could not have happened unless many had approved of it or at least had turned a blind eye to it. So it is today, where often as a

---

[14] Kidner, 'This was no exaggerated fancy. There were other Israelites scattered abroad, through whom the promises could be fulfilled', p. 69.
[15] Gen. 18:25.

result of our individualism and relativism a low spiritual temperature is tolerated and unbiblical practices become established.

The second is that only the persistent hearing and obeying the word of God can put the situation right. The ancient words of the earlier writers of Scripture which condemned earlier deviations must be listened to and heeded again.

The third is that there always must be a firm grasp on God's grace. It is in love that he gave the earlier prophetic words to snatch people out of the flames of judgment. So it was in Ezra's time and so it is today.

Ezra 10:1–44
12. Not a happy ending

It is easy to become frustrated with Bible history; we want happy endings and neatly packaged solutions. The sheer inability of God's people apparently to remember God's words is a recurring theme. Perhaps it is worse, and like Talleyrand's comment on the French aristocracy at the time of the Revolution, 'they have forgotten nothing because they know nothing'.[1] Certainly here in chapter 10 we have no happy ending, rather a catalogue of failure and unhappiness. The time is *the twentieth day of the ninth month* (v. 9) which is in the middle of winter, and the discomfort of the occasion is also underlined in the same verse with the reference to heavy rain. Yet, as we shall see, the chapter contains real hope and, as with the whole book, points to the future.

The chapter has two main sections: the peoples' confession and the action taken (vv. 1–17); and the list of those involved in intermarriage (vv. 18–44). For purposes of exposition, we shall, however, look at it in four main sections, commenting on both the flow of the story and its theological implications.

1. Hope because of the covenant (10:1–8)

The emotion in this section is unrestrained and the seriousness of the situation beyond doubt. The verbs such as *confessing*, *weeping* and *throwing himself down* do not sound like the conventional 'ordinances of religion', because most of us, in fact, do not take sin very seriously. However, this is no mere emotional display; this leads to serious and considered action which is to be the subject of the chapter.

---

[1] Attributed to Talleyrand by the Chevalier du Panat in a letter to Mallat du Pan, Jan. 1796; *Mémoires et correspondance de Mallat du Pan* [1851], 11.196.

Ezra no doubt felt at this point that he might as well have stayed in Babylon and that his efforts to teach and reform had been a failure. Now we see that this is not the case. His own seriousness and passion, far from inviting ridicule, had in fact stirred a response. Better, although the Holy Spirit is not mentioned in the chapter, he had clearly been at work in hearts and lives. This was no draconian measure forced on a reluctant community by a rigid reformer; this was an outpouring of genuine emotion – *they too wept bitterly* (v. 1) – and of sober response – *we have been unfaithful* (v. 2). The confession comes before the hope that God will be merciful.

Shecaniah, who acts as spokesman for the community, uses the phrase *in accordance with the council of my lord* (v. 3) which suggests that Ezra's words and actions had directed their decision although not specifically mandating it. This meant that the response was genuine and that it was to be thorough. This is underlined by the reference to *covenant* and *according to the Law* (v. 3). What is happening here is, in fact, a covenant renewal ceremony which echoes the great reforms of Josiah[2] and beyond that echoes Joshua's covenant renewal.[3] As we have seen so often, what is happening in Ezra flows from earlier Scriptures and shows the same God is at work. Here, something of the impact and incisiveness of Ezra's teaching of the Torah is evident. Shecaniah underwrites Ezra's leadership and urges him to take decisive action: *Rise up; this matter is in your hands. We will support you* (v. 4).

The importance of the covenant and its renewal cannot be overstated. God is faithful and, while by no means clearing the guilty, welcomes back the repentant sinner. The covenant of God is unilateral; a gift of grace to which we contribute nothing. Yet to enjoy the benefits of that covenant there needs to be response and this needs to be ongoing. Not to respond would be like going through a marriage ceremony and then saying to your spouse 'we may meet each other again some time'.

But this powerful emotional response needed to be translated into action, which expressed itself in two ways. These are summarized in the two verbs in verses 5 and 6: Ezra *rose up* and Ezra *withdrew*. The 'rising up' initiated the necessary action which involved both the leaders and the people as a whole. The further activities are summarized in verses 7–8 and show the necessity of communal confession of communal sin. Failure would attract the drastic penalty of expulsion. The province of Judah was small and Jerusalem could easily be reached from any part of it within three days. The words

[2] See 2 Chr. 34:29–31.
[3] Josh. 24:25.

used here again echo earlier Scriptures. *Forfeit* was used especially in Joshua where the city was to be 'devoted' to the Lord[4] and this involved its complete destruction. In a less drastic sense, the word could mean property given to priests.[5]

In either case, the meaning is clear. Failure to attend would involve being cut off from the community with all that this involved in being excluded from daily sacrifices and loss of rights as citizens. Although Ezra was behind this, it was a communal decision (v. 8) and thus comes with greater force.

But this action is buttressed by Ezra's withdrawing. The public prayer had spurred the people to action but now we see that this was no mere gesture. His continued prayer and fasting underlined the need for the action that was about to be taken. Prayer and action must always go together; when an immediate answer comes it is still always necessary to pray and to continue to seek God's further will and guidance.[6]

This section has focused on the true nature of the covenant relationship with the Lord. He is the injured party, the wounded Lover and no cheap or easy protestations of regret will restore that broken relationship. Only Ezra's deep and genuine confession on the peoples' behalf and the action this provoked could begin the way back to true fellowship. Underlying all this is the conviction that the only way to keep that covenant relationship alive is to follow the Torah (v. 3). That is not a gospel of good works. Rather the Lord, in his grace, has given that word to guide us through this world. This remains true in the new covenant: 'If you obey my commands, you will remain in my love, just as I have obeyed my Father's commands and remain in his love' (John 15:10); these words of Jesus are only one of many places in the New Testament where loving God in a covenant relationship is intertwined with obedience to his word.

2. Communal repentance (10:9–15)

This is a vivid and poignant little scene which shows not only a serious spiritual concern but an acute awareness of the human factors involved. The wonderful expression in verse 9, *greatly distressed by the occasion and because of the rain* encapsulates that wet, tired, uncomfortable and shaking, the people are still also trembling at the

---

[4] E.g. Josh. 6:21.

[5] E.g. Lev. 27:21.

[6] The place where Ezra prayed, *the room of Jehohanan son of Eliashib*, is one of the pointers to the relative dating of Ezra and Nehemiah. This is touched on briefly in the Introduction. For a full discussion of the issues see Kidner, Appendix IV, pp. 153–155 or Williamson (WBC), pp. 151–154.

word of God. Here is no cosy seminar but a meeting full of cross-currents of intense emotion.

The scene is set. Ezra speaks briefly and the people respond. Three elements comprise Ezra's speech. First he goes to the root of the problem: *you have been unfaithful* (v. 10). Behind this particular failure is the age-old problem of the fickleness of the human heart. Echoing 9:6, Ezra sees these marriages of foreign women as adding to the already Babel-like heap of Israel's sin. Second, he urges *confession* or more exactly 'give praise'. The phrase also occurs in Joshua 7:19 where Achan is urged to 'give glory to God'. An essential element in confession is acknowledging that God is righteous, which in effect gives him praise and accepts his verdict. Third, Ezra urges practical action. The doing of God's will in this situation will be marked by separating not just from foreign wives but from all kinds of pagan associations. We shall return to the question of what exactly is at stake here, but for the moment suffice it to say that a clear statement of principle had been made which was to be followed by decisive action.

The people's response shows both the natural human reaction and the spiritual dimension already mentioned. The ready response was no doubt a response to the drenched misery of the place, and a sensible and wise realization that precipitate action would not be the solution. However, the last phrase of verse 13, *we have sinned greatly in this thing*, is an acceptance of their culpability before the law of God.

Practicality and spirituality are both diminished when they are set in opposition to each other. Practicalities without spiritual insight can easily become unprincipled pragmatism. However, there is a kind of super-spirituality, in essence a form of Gnosticism, which denies bodily needs and ordinary emotions and leads to an unattractive legalism. Here we have attention to both the practical issues and the spiritual realities.

This resulted in a sensible and coherent programme of action. Then, as now, a large crowd is no good forum for making decisions. Thus a representative commission of *officials* (v. 14), probably the *family heads* (v. 16) would sit in Jerusalem and systematically take each village and summon those who had married foreign women. In order to be as fair as possible, these men were to be accompanied by their elders and judges who would have local knowledge relevant to the situation. But yet again the spiritual reality of God's fierce anger is the background to all this activity.

There were discordant voices and verse 15 mentions four individuals who did not give their approval to what was proposed. Since there is no comment on exactly why they opposed, or even, indeed, if *opposed this* is the correct translation, this verse has been the subject of much discussion. There are two main possible interpretations: one is that those who opposed saw the resort to divorce as too severe; the other is that they saw it as too lax and that the divorces should have been carried out summarily. The problem is that we are not told anything of the motives of these men and thus cannot tell how we are to assess their attitude.[7] We shall return briefly to this matter as well.

3. Meticulous investigation (10:16–17)

A short section now outlines how these decisions were carried out. Two matters call for comment. The first is that Ezra now takes a leading role. He was, of course, entitled to do so because of the authority given to him by the Persian king,[8] but here is called *the priest*, which shows that what he does is directed by a higher authority. This flows also from 7:1–10, where Ezra's priestly and scholarly credentials are laid out before his official authorization. Thus this must be seen as of a piece with the rest of the book where the providence of God and the activities of humans are continually intertwined.

The second is that the work both began quickly as the commission first sat only ten days after the public gathering, and its work was done meticulously as it lasted for some three months. It completed its work exactly a year after Ezra first set out from Babylon (7:9). This work cannot have been easy: winter weather may have caused delays and we have no idea how individual cases would have been handled. In any case the work was carried out, and there the narrative of Ezra effectively ends.

4. Naming and shaming (10:18–44)

Here we shall make some comments on the list of names and then examine the major issues which lie behind it, and indeed the whole of chapters 9 and 10. The list, like the others in Ezra, is carefully arranged. However, unlike the other lists, the priests are mentioned first, with the high priest's own family heading the names:

- High Priest's family (vv. 18–19)
- Other priests (vv. 20–22)
- Levites (v. 24)
- Singer and gatekeepers (v. 24)
- Laity (vv. 25–43)

[7] The linguistic and grammatical issues are set out in Fensham, p. 141 and in Williamson (WBC), pp. 156–157.

[8] See 7:25–26.

Plainly the spiritual leaders are mentioned first to underline that they should have taken the lead in righteousness and thus were more culpable. Probably the pledge and the guilt offering, although mentioned only in verse 19 in connection with the priests, should be understood as being part of the procedure for everyone.

Most commentators draw parallels with the list in chapter 2. Nine of the thirty-three families and towns of 2:3–35 reappear here, but there is no reason to argue that the list has been shortened; the practise had not extended to the entire community.

One other textual point arises in verse 44 which in the NIV reads, *All these had married foreign women, and some of them had children by these wives.*

On the basis of the parallel with 1 Esdras 9:36 many read the verse as 'All these had married foreign women, and they put them away together with their children'. This makes good sense and flows more naturally from the original decision in verse 3.[9]

Yet it is not altogether clear how we are to interpret and apply the issues raised in chapters 9 and 10. A number of points can be made. The first is that, according to Malachi 2:10–16, many Jewish men had abandoned their wives and married foreign women. This is not mentioned here, but if that were in the background, Ezra's action becomes both more readily understood and more acceptable. It would be a mistake to press this too far as we do not know if this was a relevant factor.

It has been further suggested that most of the women involved would return to their extended families. That sounds reasonable enough, but again we cannot be certain. Since the matter was investigated carefully and thoroughly (vv. 16–17) there would have been time for such arrangements to be made.

When we are looking to apply all this we remember that the New Testament explicitly rules out divorce in the case of marriage to an unbelieving partner.[10] Indeed 1 Peter 3:1–7 encourages the believing partner to live in such a way that the unbelieving partner will be attracted to the gospel.

However, when these points are made there remains a sense of uneasiness, and we may well feel with Kidner that 'the situation described in Ezra 9 and 10 was a classic example of one in which the lesser of two evils had to be chosen'.[11]

In an illuminating comment D. A. Carson points out that the

[9] Clines has a useful concise discussion, pp. 132–133.
[10] See 1 Cor. 7:12–13.
[11] Kidner, p. 71.

situation can be broadly understood in two ways.[12] The first view is that what happens here is virtually a revival which averts the anger of God and establishes the purity of the post-exilic community. The second view is that the action is inhumane and heartless and, while honouring the law which prohibits mixed marriage, dishonours the one which prohibits easy divorce and doubtless causes untold grief and distress. Carson points out that both views could be legitimate interpretations of the text. Some observations can be made.

The first is one which Carson makes himself, which is that both views contain truth. What Ezra and the community leaders did was justifiable and showed great courage in tackling a problem threatening to destroy the community. Yet there is no sign here of a heart moved with compassion or uneasiness that the action might be far too drastic. He further cites Gideon, Jephthah and Samson as examples of those in situations of complex sinfulness whose actions were less than ideal. This is an important point, and in fact a development of the observation by Kidner noted above.

A second point which follows from this is the perpetual problem of avoiding the extremes of legalism and laxity. God's people must always resist the seductive temptations of the world, the flesh and the devil. Yet it is all too easy to become legalistic and affirm doctrines which are true, but in a harsh and ungracious manner which becomes introverted and unattractive. Such a situation is reflected in John's second and third letters, where the second letter helps Christians to detect false teachers and the third warns against turning away genuine teachers. Here it would have been all too easy to have carried out the letter of the law without a truly changed heart, and Malachi witnesses to the spiritual decadence of both leaders and people. We need to remember too that this was not imposed by Ezra, it was a communal decision and carried out in the name of the leaders of the community.

A third point, which has been made several times in the course of this exposition, is that life is hard and bleak with little sign of spiritual vitality and little sign of springtime, far less the high midsummer pomps. In those circumstances, preserving the distinctiveness of the remnant from whom and to whom the Messiah would come was essential. This is where we need to see these chapters, and indeed the whole book, in the big picture. It was this dejected and downtrodden remnant, successively humbled by Persians, Greeks and Romans, that the light was to shine upon. It was to them that the sun of

---

[12] D. A. Carson, *For the Love of God*, vol. 2 (Leicester: IVP, 1999), comments for 10 January (there are no page numbers in the main body of the book; passages are found by calendar references).

righteousness was to arise with healing in his wings and the Lord was suddenly to come to his temple.[13]

Seen from that perspective Ezra as well as Haggai are lights shining in the darkness until the morning star arises. In the bigger story, Ezra is pointing to the holy city where holy people will live and God's presence will be with them continually. This remnant was the proof that God had not finished with his people and that 'the nations will know that I, the LORD, make Israel holy' (Ezek. 37:28). It lays the groundwork for the appearing of Jesus Christ. And so Ezra, like many other biblical books, ends on an unfinished note, but God's purposes continue and will one day come to fulfilment.

[13] Mal. 4:2; 3:1.

The Message of
Haggai

Introduction

It was the calling of some of the prophets to speak for God in days of great crisis. Isaiah ministered in critical years, fifty of them, which saw the rise of Assyrian imperialism, the fall and exile of the northern kingdom of Israel and the miraculous rescue of Judah. Habakkuk spoke on the very brink of exile and saw the rise of neo-Babylonian power. Haggai faced in some ways a more trying situation; a time of inertia and apathy when spiritual life had burned low and a relatively settled political situation and a fair degree of comfort had resulted in a disinclination to hear the word of God and act upon it.

The background to the prophecy is the return from exile in 538 BC following the downfall of the Babylonian Empire at the hands of the Persian Cyrus in 539 BC.[1] Haggai and Zechariah speak into the situation where the early pioneers who had begun to rebuild the temple as shown in Ezra 1 – 3, had ceased to do so because of a combination of external opposition and internal failure of nerve.[2] Haggai's message is brief and delivered in a period of under four months. Yet his prophecy deals, as we shall see, with huge issues and led to a fundamental change of heart and life among those to whom it was delivered.

1. Who was he?

In terms of the individual we know nothing except this short book and brief mentions in Ezra 5:1–2 and 6:14. We do not know if he was born in Babylon and returned to Jerusalem with the first group of exiles (his referring to the *house in its former glory* in 2:3 is hardly evidence that he was now old). Similarly, his references to the laws of holiness in 2:11–13 hardly proves he was a priest, since these were straightforward regulations known to nearly everyone.

[1] See the Introduction to Ezra.
[2] See Ezra 4.

However, what is more significant is that he is a *prophet* (1:1; 2:1, 10) and *the LORD's messenger* (1:13). The fact that he is simply called *the prophet Haggai* suggests that he was well known and needed no other identification. The fact that he had a word from the Lord was more important than his family background, age or other circumstances. The message he brought was hugely significant in the unfolding story of God's people. He and Zechariah were used by God to prevent the return from exile being a pointless journey and the rebuilding of the temple a monument to beginning a work which was not completed. The term *prophet* is reinforced by the term *messenger*, which emphasizes the divine origin of the word Haggai brings.

2. What was his message?

The basic simplicity and directness of Haggai's message should not be allowed to obscure the magnitude of the issues with which he is concerned. Further, he stands in the mainstream prophetic tradition as it flows from Moses and the exodus events[3] as well as in his commitment to the Davidic house and its future. Five main emphases can be discerned.

a. The word of God

We have already noted the description of Haggai as *prophet* and *messenger*. There is also extensive use of the 'messenger formula'. It is common for prophets to introduce their oracles with a phrase like 'thus says the Lord', but Haggai often also concludes with this (2:7, 9, 23) and sometimes repeats it in the middle (e.g. 2:4). The book concludes with the phrase *declares the LORD Almighty*. This emphasis on the word of God has two effects.

One is that Haggai is not giving his private analysis of the situation. He speaks with the authority of a messenger from the Lord of hosts,[4] a word which relativizes all other words. His words, therefore, come with the authority of the revelation given to and through Moses and in the direct line of that teaching.

The other is that the words are those of Haggai. He does not make up the message but the style and accent are his own.[5] He is a direct and forthright speaker; Joyce Baldwin compares him to Elijah.[6] He is fond of such words as 'consider' (ESV) (*give careful thought*, NIV,

---

[3] See 2:5.
[4] See the exposition of Hag. 1:1–2, below.
[5] See 'Structure and style', below.
[6] Baldwin, p. 31.

1:5, 7; 2:15, 18) which show he is not calling for unreflecting action but a total commitment of heart and mind to the Lord.

b. The temple

Some have found this emphasis on the building of the temple to be narrow and confining, and evidence of a ritualistic and even superstitious attitude. But that is a superficial reading of the text. This can be seen when we look at 2:4–5: 'For I am with you, declares the LORD Almighty. "This is what I covenanted with you when you came out of Egypt."' The reference here to God's presence among his people is embodied in the commands to build a tabernacle: 'Have them make a sanctuary for me, and I will dwell among them' (Exod. 25:8; see Exod. 29:45–46). This command remained valid, and failure to rebuild the temple would have been tantamount to saying that they did not want God dwelling among them or at least that they did not care. Far from being a ritualistic and legalistic activity, the building of the temple and the accompanying sacrifices was a response to grace.

It is significant that so much time is spent in Exodus 26 – 27 specifying the way in which the tent was to be constructed. Similarly, in 1 Kings 6 – 8 (and even more in 1 Chr. 28 – 2 Chr. 7) the construction of the temple is dwelt on. The obedience involved in following God's commands to build a house is an act of faith that God would keep his promise to dwell with them. Thus the temple was not a cultic centre but a place where God whom 'the highest heaven' cannot contain (1 Kgs 8:27) was pleased to dwell and be among his people.

c. Messianic hope

As well as the link with Moses, Haggai emphasizes the importance of the Davidic kingship and the covenant with David in 2 Samuel 7. The call to build comes to Zerubbabel, who we learn in 1 Chronicles 3:19 was grandson of Jehoiachin, one of the last kings of David's line to reign in Jerusalem. This forms an *inclusio* with 2:20–23 where the promises made to David in 2 Samuel 7 are to be fulfilled in Zerubbabel.[7]

The link with David and the temple is clear in 2 Samuel 7. David expressed to Nathan his desire to build a temple for the Lord (v. 2). However, Nathan brings the message that it is the Lord who will build a house for David (v. 11). This house is to be the Davidic dynasty which is to be established for ever.

[7] See 'Eschatology', below.

d. Covenant

Haggai stands in the mainstream of Israel's life and faith. The word 'covenant' indeed is mentioned only in 2:5[8] where the presence of God, manifested at the exodus, remains among them to bless and to judge. But there is much more than that. Yahweh, the covenant name, occurs thirty-four times. Moreover, the physical hardships of 1:5–6 and 2:16–17 echo the words of Amos 4:6–10 which themselves echo the curses for covenant disobedience of Deuteronomy 28. Haggai's call to action is covenantal through and through.

But there is more. Haggai's calling as a prophet places him firmly in succession from Moses. Moses is the fountainhead of Old Testament revelation and the unique prophet whom God knew face to face.[9] Through him was given the Torah (Pentateuch). The words of Moses are the words of God; there is no revelation in Old Testament times which is superior to and independent of that given to Moses. Thus the prophets were raised up to call people back to the message given to Moses as the way to build godly lives and flourishing communities. This makes the message of Haggai relevant to his time and all times, for it is the living word of God.

e. Eschatology

Haggai is able to speak to all times including his own because his perspective is primarily an eschatological one. The temple-building project is to conclude when the Lord will fill the temple with glory (2:7). Similarly, and in far greater detail, Ezekiel pictures the restored temple with the prince living there.[10] The covenant blessings culminate in a Messianic figure who will reign on David's throne. Paul sees this being fulfilled as the nations come in faith and obedience to the 'Root of Jesse . . . who will arise to rule over the nations' (Rom. 15:12).

The guarantee of all this future glory was the present activity of the Spirit (2:5). Haggai, as he saw the apathy and unbelief of his own day turned to obedience and faith by the preaching of the word, anticipated that coming day.

3. Structure and style

The book shows evidence of careful editorial arrangement, almost certainly by Haggai himself. It consists of a series of six oracles

---

[8] We may compare this with earlier prophets.
[9] Deut. 34:10.
[10] Ezek. 40 – 48.

carefully arranged both chronologically and theologically. The chronology is as follows, with the events falling in *the second year of Darius I*:

1:1	*first day of the sixth month*	29 August 520 BC
1:15	*twenty-fourth day of the sixth month*	21 September 520 BC
2:1	*twenty-first day of the seventh month*	17 October 520 BC
2:15	*twenty-fourth day of the ninth month*	18 December 520 BC
2:20	*a second time on the twenty-fourth day of the ninth month*	

The period is brief – a little under four months – but the effectiveness of a ministry does not depend on its length.

The arrangement, however, is not simply time-conditioned; there is a real progression of thought. The book begins (1:1–2, 3–11) and ends (2:10–19, 20–23) with two oracles each on the same day addressed to leaders and people. In the middle are two oracles (1:12–15; 2:1–19), each of which emphasize the Lord's presence – *I am with you* (1:13; 2:4). The movement is from rebuke to call for action, to encouragement and to promise. The importance of the Davidic connection is underlined by the *inclusio* of the mention of Zerubbabel (1:1; 2:23) and the eschatological perspective of the later reference.

Haggai's style is brisk and wastes no words. Yet we should resist the temptation to see him as a practical man compared to the visionary Zechariah. It is true that Haggai lacks the soaring apocalyptic visions of Zechariah but we shall see (as with Ezra) his echoes of earlier Scripture giving a rich and vital thrust to his writing as well as his eschatological passages. The movement of prophetic word leading to repentance, to action and to blessing is central to the flow of the book.

As we work our way through the book we shall use these six oracles as the basis for exposition, and trace the flow of the prophecy as well as dwell on details.

Haggai 1:1–2
1. When are we to build?

Some people or institutions are perpetually disadvantaged by being overshadowed by someone or something appearing to be more glamorous or interesting. They are seldom mentioned on their own but simply as an appendage to their more impressive companion. Thus Boswell is the biographer of Dr Johnson rather than being valued for his own sake. It happens with churches where a prosperous work in the suburbs with plenty of support and the oxygen of publicity overshadows a struggling group in the inner city. Haggai the prophet, similarly, seems tiny and unimpressive in the shadow of the splendours of Zechariah. But Haggai is small only in length; he has hugely important things to say, and even in these first two verses great issues and vital principles are established. Four matters deserve our attention.

1. When Haggai prophesied

The precise dating and circumstances in verse 1 are characteristic of Scripture. God's voice comes to actual people where they are and speaks in language specifically addressed to that situation. The Darius here is the first, known as Hystaspes, who in his early months was preoccupied with putting down rebellion, but now is secure in his rule. The year is 520 BC and the actual time is the first day of the sixth month: late August at the time of fruit harvest. That was a time of special offerings[1] and these would be a reminder of the unfinished project. The altar had indeed been built but the failure to persevere with the temple would inevitably raise question marks about the sincerity and validity of such offerings.

The prophet first addresses the leaders, Zerubbabel and Joshua. We have already encountered these men in the early chapters of Ezra

[1] See Num. 28:11–15.

and seen how in Ezra 5:1–2 they took a lead in responding to Haggai as they had already been leaders of the first group of returning exiles. Prophetic ministry addresses both leaders and people; sometimes one or the other being given more attention. Thus Isaiah begins with the sinful nation and moves swiftly to the 'rulers of Sodom' and 'people of Gomorrah'.[2] Malachi speaks first to people and then to priests. Here Haggai begins with the leaders who need to take the initiative if the task is to be resumed.

Thus the call is specific and to particular people but, as we shall see, it is about a collective issue. It is just this blend of the local and occasional with the big picture which gives the prophetic writings, indeed all Scripture, their capacity to speak from their own age into every age. Before he is done, Haggai is going to take us from this low-key situation in Jerusalem to the shaking of heaven and earth and the coming of God's kingdom.

2. What his calling was

Haggai is called *the prophet*.[3] This instantly links him with Moses[4] and tells us that he is going to be a messenger of the covenant and call the people back to faithfulness to the covenant Lord. Habakkuk and Zechariah are also so designated.[5] It is surely significant that Haggai is seven times so described (Hag. 1:1, 3, 12; 2:1; see Ezra 5:1; 6:14). His message may have been brief but his authority is not in doubt. Yet that authority is not some status given by an official position, rather it was a direct calling and gifting from Yahweh himself.

That authority is expressed in the phrase: *the word of the LORD came through the prophet Haggai* (1:1). More literally the phrase reads 'the word came . . . by the hand of', rather than the more common 'the word of the LORD came to'. The 'came' is supplied in the English translations; the verb used in Hebrew is the verb 'to be', with its connotations of the word being part of, indeed becoming flesh in the prophet. This is most dramatically conveyed when Ezekiel eats the scroll.[6] For the prophet the word of God is something so much part of them that whether pleasant or painful it must be spoken.[7] This is the word which Isaiah says will not fail to accomplish its purpose.[8]

[2] Isa. 1:4, 10.
[3] Baldwin, p. 28.
[4] Deut. 18:18–20.
[5] Hab. 1:1; Zech. 1:1.
[6] Ezek. 3:1–3.
[7] See Jer. 20:9.
[8] Isa. 55:10–11.

Nothing is said of how this revelation comes, but the fact that it is revelation and not speculation or opinion is emphasized. The living word does its work unseen but its results are seen in transformation as well as in judgment. The result is that what we have is the word of the Lord through the words of Haggai. God's characteristic way of dealing with both idolatry and apathy among his people is to send prophets, and Haggai no less than Elijah brings that word into a situation which badly needs it. 'Thus says' is the common phrase for the contents of the prophet's message, and the use of the perfect tense emphasizes the decisiveness of what is said.[9]

The source of the message here is 'the LORD of hosts',[10] a title frequent in the prophets and not least in Haggai, Zechariah and Malachi. Its first occurrences are in 1 Samuel: at 1:3 referring to the worship of the Lord at Shiloh; again in Hannah's prayer and in reference to the ark.[11] The word $ṣĕbā'ôt$, 'hosts', is reflected in the Latin *Dominus exercituum*, 'Lord of armies'. The word is probably best understood as a plural denoting the presence in God of every source of power and authority, as well as Lord of all the powers in heaven and earth. The hosts are probably the angel armies, the heavenly court[12] and as such the title may reflect the access the prophet is given to that court and that he comes from it with the authoritative word. In any case, the title emphasizes the invincible authority of God's word and the certainty of its fulfilment.

3. What his message is

The first message is brief and blunt: *These people say, 'The time has not yet come for the LORD's house to be built'* (v. 2). The first thing to notice is the phrase *these people*. This is deliberately neutral, although Baldwin sees it as a rebuke.[13] What it does show is the importance of the response to the Lord's word. How they respond will determine whether the designation 'my people' is a deserved one or whether they want to disassociate themselves from God. True prophets are always calling for repentance and change and Haggai is taking nothing for granted.

[9] Motyer, 'Haggai', says 'It is not that the Lord spoke thus at some time in the past but that this is his definitive present utterance', p. 974.

[10] It is unfortunate that the NIV always renders the phrase as 'the LORD Almighty' which obscures the nuances of meaning. Probably it is reflecting the LXX rendering – *kyrios pantokratōr*.

[11] 1 Sam. 1:11; 4:4.

[12] E.g. Ps. 103:20–21; Isa. 6:1–6.

[13] Baldwin, p. 39.

The time has not yet come encapsulates the spirit of apathy and defeatism which had gripped the people. What they were in fact saying was that the time will never come. They were accepting this state of spiritual deadness as normal. We are to learn in the next few verses that the people were assiduous in pursuing their own comforts and employment, but that enthusiasm and activity did not extend to their spiritual health and vitality. The 'time' here is translated by Motyer as 'the right time', and he compares this to the Greek *kairos*.[14] The emphasis is spiritual rather than chronological. These people knew that the time had arrived. Ezra 1:1 shows that it was not simply the decree of Cyrus but the hand of God which had brought them back to the land. However, they had allowed external forces and low morale to lead to their abandoning the building of the temple and their loyalty to God had withered.

The only antidote to this is the living word. This underlines the importance of the precise dating of the first message from Haggai. The people were allowing time to drift past, but God speaks to them in the urgency of the present moment. This emphasis on the immediate relevance of God's word is underlined in Psalm 95:7–8: 'Today if you hear his voice, do not harden your hearts.' Hebrews 3:13, picking this up, urges obedience 'as long as it is called Today'. The word of God is always speaking to us where we are and urging us to new commitment.

It is not clear where this message is delivered. Some commentators believe that the prophet may have visited the site and spoken there, perhaps gesturing towards other people – *these people*. In any case his language has the vividness of an actual account and shows an instinct for what will make an immediate impact.

4. The Lord's house

The Lord's house is in the emphatic position which cannot easily be replicated in English but there is no doubt of its importance to Haggai. Comment has already been made in the introduction and in the exposition of the early chapters of Ezra on the temple and its significance, but a number of things can be said here. The temple is more than another way of saying put God first, that is axiomatic. Rather it is putting the presence of God at the centre of his people.

We know from Ezra 4 of the external opposition to the building of the temple but Haggai does not focus on this. Rather he goes to the root of the problem, which is that the people's hearts had grown cold and they were not giving priority to God's presence among them.

[14] Motyer, 'Haggai', p. 974.

a. They had lost faith in God's covenant

The fact that the covenant name Yahweh is used shows that at heart is the covenant God made with his people. The exile had not destroyed that, but mere return from Babylon would not restore ancient glories, and repentance and commitment in the present were needed. Without that they might be as well in Babylon since they were neglecting the whole reason for their return. The building of the sanctuary was to be evidence that God's covenant was in place and that his purposes of redemption had not been set aside.

b. They had lost the desire to meet God in the present

The tragedy of the exile was only partly the removal of the people from the land and the destruction of city and temple. The real tragedy was the departure of the indwelling glory of God which Ezekiel depicts so poignantly in chapter 10 of his prophecy. Without the return of God's glory the place would remain unsanctified and blessing would not come. The prophetic voice of Haggai is a sign that the Lord still has purposes of grace, but to enjoy these his people need to prepare a place for him.

c. They had no vision for the future

Later Haggai is to speak of the amazing ingathering of the peoples and of the wealth of the nations to the restored temple. But that glorious vision is obscured by the present reality: an altar surrounded by the rubble of unfinished building. How little sign there was that God's glory would be revealed and we are inclined to ask why the actual return should be so low key. O. Palmer Robertson, in his fine book, *The Christ of the Prophets*, among many other sharp observations on the prophets of the restoration says this: 'This coming anointed one of the restoration prophets is to appear in a state of humiliation so that he might fulfil the previously described role of the suffering servant of the Lord.'[15] Thus there could be no glorious Davidic king reigning in a restored kingdom before the coming priest/king suffered.

Thus the challenge to rebuild the temple goes far beyond a mere restoration and is much more significant than erecting a building. That was vital as a sign that God's redemptive purposes were continuing and that, in spite of meagre evidence, the glory of the temple would not be limited to a physical structure.

[15] Robertson, p. 366.

In two brief verses Haggai has established his credentials and given the essence of his message. There is much here for us to learn. If we want to inspire people to rebuild the Lord's temple we will do that only as we are faithful to the living word. The emphasis will not be so much on programmes and strategies as on unleashing that word and allowing it to do its appointed work. We shall see how that word breathes life back into the embers.

Haggai 1:3–11
2. A wake-up call

Here Haggai's opening words are expanded into an analysis of the situation in terms of both its material and spiritual realities. Again there is the emphasis on the fact that this is a word from the Lord, not only in verse 3, but again in verses 5, 7, 8 and 9. Perhaps here we have a summary of much fuller oracles which the prophet spoke on that occasion. The words are both pointed and memorable in themselves and a model of how to proclaim and apply the word of God.

The structure is clear and lucid and we shall use that as a basis for the exposition. Haggai's 'wake-up call' develops as a number of specific appeals.

- Appeal to priorities (vv. 3–4): visual evidence of the people's failure.
- Appeal to see the reality of their situation (vv. 5–6): they have all the basic necessities of life but lack satisfaction.
- Appeal to thought and action (vv. 7–8): they need to reflect on God's word and take action as a result.
- Appeal to see what lies behind their situation (vv. 9–11): they have ignored God as well as their own Scriptures and history.

Haggai begins with the specific situation, moves to the people's own concerns and shows how their disobedience has badly affected the quality of their lives.

1. Appeal to priorities (1:3–4)

Haggai's question contrasts *your houses* with *this house* and the *panelled* nature of their own with the ruined state of Yahweh's. *You yourselves* emphasizes their own preoccupation with themselves which is further underlined by the word translated *panelled*. There is the suggestion of elegance, even luxury, which sits uneasily with the rubble and debris of the temple mound. It was not lack of money but lack of will which prevented the building of Yahweh's house. Baldwin pointedly comments: 'The conflict of expenditure on luxury homes and worthy support of God's work is still with us'.[1] Haggai, having caught their attention with this pointed comment, now goes on to develop its implications.

2. Appeal to see the reality of their situation (1:5–6)

The people had compartmentalized their lives: one part (the larger) for themselves and the remainder for Yahweh. Haggai now shows them that this is impossible, for there is actually no part of their lives where they can hide from God. The prophet speaks of eating, drinking and clothes which are at once the basic necessities of life and stand for the whole of material existence including the *panelled houses*. Similarly the planting and harvesting encapsulate the basic work of an agricultural economy.

Here we have material prosperity and security without any real fulfilment, a situation somewhat like that envisaged in Ecclesiastes 1:8: 'All things are wearisome, more than one can say. The eye never has enough of seeing, nor the ear its fill of hearing.' They are not in poverty, they are comfortable, but they are profoundly dissatisfied.

Haggai calls them to *give careful thought* (NIV), to 'consider' (ESV). The expression literally means 'set your heart upon' and implies serious reflection which looks beyond the surface to find the underlying cause of their dissatisfaction. *Your ways* refers to their whole lifestyle and where it was going, and called them to look beyond the present. Nor was this simply an intellectual exercise, it was a calling for a response to the Lord's word through Haggai which, as we shall see, echoes the words of Moses. It is, in fact, a call to think biblically and to allow God to govern their lives. Change will not come by idle feelings but by vigorous and purposeful engagement with the word of God.

3. Appeal to thought and action (1:7–8)

The call to consider is repeated and this is coupled with a call to action. Haggai is not urging them to become contemplatives, rather to reflect deeply and then act. Action without reflection is usually unwise but reflection without action is sterile. Haggai wants

---

[1] Baldwin, p. 40.

to see evidence that the word of Yahweh is at work in the people's lives.

The particular action is to climb the mountains and bring wood for the rebuilding. Nehemiah 8:15 speaks of the abundant trees in the hill country. The important thing is to *build the house* for God's pleasure and honour. To rebuild the temple would be a tangible demonstration of the people's desire for God to be with them again. The glory of the Lord does not depend on the magnificence of the structure but on the fact that God is there, just as a nameless place became for Jacob the house of God and the gate of heaven.[2]

This lifts everything on to a higher plane. The hard work of getting timber and beginning again the task of building would be unglamorous and laborious. Yet the compensation far outweighed the effort: in the present Yahweh returning to live among his people, and in the future a glorious temple to which all the nations would come.

4. Appeal to see what lies behind their situation (1:9–11)

Now Haggai spells out the reason why things are the way they are: they have failed to honour God by rebuilding his house and he is punishing them. Behind all secondary causes lies the providence of God. Here he is echoing words of earlier prophets and reinforcing the conviction that Yahweh is not some godlet but the universal Lord. Negatively here Haggai is asserting what is said positively in Psalm 121:2: 'My help comes from the LORD, the Maker of heaven and earth.'

Ultimately at stake is whether people actually believe in this God who not only made heaven and earth but continues to be involved as he uses all that he has made to fulfil his purpose. Once again the Psalms express this vividly: 'Lightning and hail, snow and clouds, stormy winds that do his bidding' (Ps. 148:8). *I called for a drought* (v. 11) reflects Amos 4:6–9, which itself reflects the covenant curses of Deuteronomy 28:38–42. If such a God exists then plainly we cannot be only partly related to him and exclude him from certain parts of our life (usually the most important ones). Just as the Lord had brought the exile[3] and reversed it[4] now he was still acting sovereignly. He was acting in judgment in affecting the basic necessities of living, but he was also acting in mercy in sending a prophet to open their eyes to the reality of the situation.

Covenant language is striking in verse 10 when heaven and earth (whom Moses calls to witness in Deut. 4:26 and Isaiah echoes in 1:2)

[2] Gen. 28:17.
[3] Dan. 1:1–2.
[4] Ezra 1:1.

are summoned by the Creator to show his displeasure with his people. Moreover, in Deuteronomy 28:12 the bounty of the heavens is explicitly linked with obedience to God's commands. Indeed, in that verse, heaven is described as a storehouse of the Lord's bounty. In a later generation, Malachi is to use a similar image of the Lord opening the floodgates of heaven in response to the people's commitment.[5]

Beyond that there is a clear link with Genesis 3:17: 'Cursed is the ground because of you.' What is happening here in Haggai's day is another evidence of the outworking of that curse; this is not bad economic management or failure of agricultural method, it is a direct judgment of the Creator. The theological message of the prophet is in the mainstream of biblical revelation. Any idea that his message is narrow and localized cannot be sustained when we study this kind of passage. Israel's God is the Creator and the Lord of history, and his people's disobedience strikes at the very heart of their covenant faith.

This is no theoretical failure: *Because of my house which remains a ruin, while each of you is busy with his own house* (v. 9). Wordplay in the Hebrew text reinforces the link between the drought and the failure to build the Lord's house.[6] What they had placed at the margins of their lives proves to be central in its impact and until the Lord is given first place nothing will go right. Later Haggai is to show the positive blessings which will flow when true loyalty is restored.

In some ways this first direct address of Haggai is fairly straightforward and uncomplicated but there are many issues to ponder more deeply especially as he speaks beyond his time to focus on matter which still concern the church deeply. It is to these broader issues we now return.

5. Haggai as a preacher

Verses 3–11 give us an example of Haggai's preaching ministry and a model of what true preaching is. Haggai begins with a pointed address to the specific situations, expands this into a wider picture of their whole lives and appeals for action on the basis of their whole worldview drawn from their Scriptures. These are the elements of all good preaching, not always in the same order, and often in different proportions and combinations, and it is interesting to see how Haggai blends these into his sermon here.

[5] Mal. 3:10.
[6] *ḥāreb* ('ruin') and *ḥōreb* ('drought') underline that the one is the cause of the other.

The first thing to notice is how Haggai's words are direct and pointed. No generalization about putting God first, rather a specific contrast between the state of God's house and their houses. The evidence was unmistakeable and right in front of their eyes. All too often application is left vague and unspecified and thus fails completely.

Then we see how he expands this specific issue into a commentary which goes to the root of their attitude and lifestyle. Haggai, like the good preacher he is, gets underneath the people's defences, as they were probably thinking that the temple had little to do with what really mattered to them. However, by showing that every part of life is affected by this failure he ensures their attention. Moreover he points out the remedy both in a change of attitude and the resulting renewed action.

All this could easily suggest that Haggai is simply moralizing or giving a pep talk. But the repeated emphasis on the word of the Lord and the echoes of earlier Scriptures show that the Lord is again communicating with his people. Haggai is the first prophetic voice to the returned exiles and that is a sign that God still has purposes for his people. Here the prophet's voice is a wake-up call, a word of challenge and rebuke. We are about to see Haggai giving a message of encouragement and the same elements which marked the rebuke are also present in the comfort.

6. The use of Scripture

The straightforward message of Haggai gains power and depth, not only from his speaking as the mouthpiece of God, but from the echoes of earlier Scriptures. These give us a glimpse of the big picture and a sense of the ongoing purposes of God. It is fascinating to reflect on the prophet's use of earlier Scripture, and a number of things can be said.

The first is that Haggai presupposes the existence of the Pentateuch. The basic theology of the dwelling of God with his people and the sacrificial system lie behind what he says.[7] He has clearly meditated on the later chapters of Exodus and the book of Leviticus and he plainly expects the people to understand this. Thus his exhortations are totally in line with the fountainhead of prophetic revelation, Moses himself. Baldwin points out that his method echoes that of Moses reflecting in Deuteronomy on the exodus events.[8]

[7] See Ezra 3.
[8] Baldwin, p. 40.

It is indeed the covenant curses of Deuteronomy 28 which are reflected in verses 7–11 and remind us of that book's stark contrast of the ways of life and death.[9] Moreover, the principle to which Haggai appeals of the total sovereignty of the Lord over life, work and the whole of creation is encapsulated in Deuteronomy 8:18: 'But remember the LORD your God, for it is he who gives you the ability to produce wealth, and so confirms his covenant, which he swore to your forefathers, as it is today.'

This, with Haggai's words here, underlines the divine grace which is the nature of God as much in the Old Testament as the New Testament. We can no more achieve anything in the material world without the gift of God than we can save ourselves.

We have seen how Haggai uses these two themes of creation and history to show the seriousness of his message. This emphasizes the importance of the temple in the overall picture. It is linked with creation, when God walked in the Garden of Eden, and finally with new creation, when the dwelling of God will be with humans. This is what the story is about: the temple, and before that the tabernacle, were at the heart of the people, and if they were not, disaster quickly followed.

7. The state of the people

One of the reasons why Haggai seems less colourful and dramatic than earlier prophets is the nature of the sin he is condemning. There are no colourful denunciations of bogus religion and social injustice as in Amos; no powerful condemnations of idolatry as in Isaiah and Jeremiah, nor the passionate appeals of Hosea. Rather what Haggai faces is a complacent apathy which manifests itself in a chilling indifference to the Lord. It is fascinating to compare this with the letters to the seven churches in Revelation 2 and 3. The severest condemnation comes to Laodicea.[10] Did Laodicea have worse heresies than Pergamum who held to the teaching of Balaam or Thyatira who 'tolerated that woman Jezebel'?[11] Were its immoralities more serious than Thyatira with its sexual license?[12] Laodicea has none of those things because in Laodicea there was not enough life for such weeds to take root and grow. Rather the tepid and complacent nature of the church made it an offence. So it is here, and so it is always. Here, as in Revelation, it is only the living word

[9] Deut. 30:19.
[10] Rev. 3:14–22.
[11] Rev. 2:14, 20.
[12] Rev. 2:20.

of God by the power of the Spirit which can transform people's hearts.

The prophets were never simply concerned with outward failures and obvious sins, they were primarily concerned with the covenant and all that implied of heart devotion and true commitment to the Lord from which everything else flowed. This meant that anything less than having the Lord at the centre of their lives and their community was as damaging as idolatry; indeed we can see the consequences of the attitude Haggai castigates here half a century later in the book of Malachi.

8. The temple itself

Probably no part of Scripture reveals so clearly the importance of the temple as the outward sign that God was living among his people. It was not that stone and wood had a significance in themselves: to think that was idolatry.[13] Nor even that the sacrificial system was meritorious in itself,[14] but both manifested commitment to the Lord whose holiness dwelt among them. Until Jesus died outside the sacred enclosure these visible and acted parables are part of the divinely ordered way to express the reality of the presence of the living God.

When the temple building was a ruin life could still continue, as it ticks over in many a congregation where the Bible no longer sets the agenda and the flames of love and faith have burned low. And when that happens, as in the case of Laodicea, that church is on the verge of extinction. But there is something more sinister at work here.[15] Satan is again attempting to destroy the work of God and prevent by any means he can the coming of the one who is the true temple and 'God's presence and his very self'.[16]

---

[13] See e.g. Isa. 40:19–20; Jer. 10:7–10.
[14] See e.g. Amos 5:21–27.
[15] See above on Ezra 4.
[16] From J. H. Newman, hymn: 'Praise to the holiest in the height', 1865.

Haggai 1:12–15
3. At the centre

The fundamental problem up to now had not been disbelief in God, nor had it been idolatry; rather God, who ought to have been at the centre, had been pushed to the margins. What happens now is a transformation of both the leaders and the people which changes the situation profoundly. The difference is that the word of God had broken through the complacency, stirred and challenged hearts and the Spirit of God was powerfully at work. The passage develops in three movements: obedience (v. 12); reassurance (v. 13); divine and human action (vv. 14–15).

1. Obedience (v. 12)

There are not many examples of the words of a prophet being heeded so swiftly and spectacularly.[1] Here leaders and people are moved to obedience and subsequently to action. This was a thorough change. The people are not now *these people* but the *whole remnant of the people*.[2] These are the people who have not only physically returned to the land, but those who have returned to the Lord. The word *šûb* 'return' is a common term in the prophets calling on the people to turn back to the Lord in repentance and faith, and this is what is happening here.

This 'returning' is shown by their obedience, which is in itself a work of God who had sent Haggai to them. The words used here are fascinating. What they obeyed was the *voice of the LORD* which came to them through the 'words' (ESV) or *message* (NIV) of Haggai. A similar idea occurs in Acts 10:44 in the account of Peter speaking at Cornelius' house: 'While Peter was still speaking these words, the

---

[1] Jonah is a clear example; also David's response to Nathan (2 Sam. 12:13).
[2] See further the comments on Ezra 1, above.

Holy Spirit came on all who heard the message.' Neither in Haggai nor Acts is the divine word collapsed into the human word, but in both the words of the human messenger are the voice of the Lord himself.[3] Similarly here, the people of that time recognized the words of Haggai as the word of God and responded in obedience.

Their response is further shown by the description of God as *the LORD their God*. This not only underlines God's grace but their renewed relationship with him. Their conviction that Haggai was the Lord's messenger is a pleasing contrast to the hostility shown to so many of the prophets. The returning to the Lord was nothing less than the fear of the Lord which is the beginning of wisdom.[4] They now tremble at the word of God; an attitude which Isaiah sees as fulfilling the condition for his dwelling with people.[5]

2. Reassurance (v. 13)

What is striking here is the new title given to Haggai – *the LORD's messenger* – and the emphasis on what he says as *the message of the LORD*. This does not show the verse in an interpolation as some have argued; rather it shows a new awareness on the part of the people that the words they were hearing were the words of the living God. As we have seen, these are also the words of Haggai (and could not, for example, easily be mistaken for those of Zechariah) but their impact is now life-changing.

His new message is one of encouragement and reassurance which not only echoes earlier Scriptures but is perfectly adapted to the specific situation. Baldwin[6] points out that Haggai may have been referring to Isaiah 42:18 – 43:7 where the return from exile is predicted and the words 'Do not be afraid, for I am with you' (43:5) occur. That may be, but the phrase is also used for Jacob (Gen. 28:15) and Moses (Exod. 3:12). It is the assurance that God has committed himself to them.

But more than that is implied. God being with them was bound up with rebuilding his house, not simply in terms of wood and stone but in terms of changed hearts which responded to his word. This word was also assurance of protection against the opposition we read of in Ezra 4 and 5. It was a reassurance that the work would be done because they were not doing it in their own energies. Thus the word of exhortation and rebuke is followed by the word of encouragement and invigoration.

[3] Motyer, 'Haggai' comments: 'The articulation is human, the voice divine.'
[4] Ps. 111:10.
[5] Isa. 66:1–2.
[6] Baldwin, p. 43.

3. Divine and human action (vv. 14–15)

The words of the prophet are the audible sign of the divine activity in the hearts of both leaders and people. *The LORD stirred up*; the continuity of God's purposes is shown by the use of the same verb in Ezra 1, first of Cyrus (v. 1) and then the leaders of the people (v. 5). This also anticipates 2:5 where the Spirit of God is mentioned. Here it is not only the civic and religious leaders but the whole remnant of the people. This is a striking example of the fact that the Lord's passion for his glory and the blessing of his people does not wax and wane according to their feelings.

The divine activity results in human action: *They came and began to work on the house of the LORD.* Much remains to be done, but the centrality of the indwelling LORD is now established and it is time to get the project begun. Commentators draw attention to the twenty-three days that elapsed between Haggai's message of 1:1 and 1:3 and the resumption of work on *the twenty-fourth day of the sixth month*. This betrays little understanding of the human and logistical factors involved. Teams would have to be organized, materials prepared, detailed specifications worked out; and since the site had been abandoned for twenty years much rubbish would have accumulated. The harvest was also gathered in the sixth month, and could not simply be left. The important thing was the change of heart which led to the renewed activity.

4. A note on 1:15b

In modern translations the phrase *in the second year of King Darius* is regarded as the end of chapter 1 rather than the beginning of chapter 2. Some have argued that 1:15 should be followed by 2:15–19, arguing that 2:10–14 has little connection with verses 15–19. That view is unsustainable (see exposition of relevant verses).

It seems more likely that *in the second year of Darius* belongs with chapter 2 and introduces the second group of oracles. It is often argued that the expression *laḥōdeš baššiššî*, 'of the month, in the sixth', is odd because of the construction of a number with the definite article and the preposition 'be'.[7] Moreover, the echo of 1:1 seems unmistakeable. The book is carefully crafted, and unnecessary rearrangements such as the moving of 2:15–19 should be avoided.

---

[7] Note, however, a similar construction in Ezek. 1:1.

5. General comments

Haggai's brief word had been spectacularly effective and work has begun on the temple. Although we must suppose that what we have here is a concise summary of Haggai's words, his message is brief and pointed. It would be useful to reflect now on some of the major issues touched on in the exposition of chapter 1 and see something of the significance of the chapter as a whole.

a. The word of God

This brief chapter is one of the most significant in the Bible for seeing and studying the effect of the word of God both in terms of its delivery and its reception. We have an unusually comprehensive, although brief, presentation of how that word is received by the prophet, heard by the people and then acted upon. This is a striking illustration of Isaiah 55:11: 'my word that goes out from my mouth: it will not return to me empty, but will accomplish what I desire and achieve the purpose for which I sent it.' Here we can examine that at its most elemental and most striking.

The first element is the mystery of the givenness of the divine word. Mystery does not mean vagueness: this word is given at a time which is precisely dated. The mystery is rather that the divine word comes unasked and unassisted by humans and accomplishes its work of transforming or of judgment, and nothing can prevent that. Haggai did not decide, after private investigation, that the word of God was needed but, under the compulsion of the Spirit, he became the willing messenger. Why it should be this man, about whom nothing else is known, is part of the mystery.

This is the next element: the messenger himself. Some prophets, notably Jeremiah, are shown wrestling with the message[8] before delivering it faithfully. Here we have nothing about how Haggai felt about what he was given to say but are only shown his total commitment to delivering it. Ultimately this is what distinguishes a true messenger of the Lord, and Haggai shows us that reality stripped of any personal circumstances or problems surrounding it. We would have been greatly impoverished without the insights into the personal circumstances of Jeremiah or the agonies and ecstasies of Ezekiel. What Haggai gives us is the divine imperative to preach the word and the divine assurance that the word will do its work.

The next element is the nature of the prophetic word. We have already noticed how Haggai moves from rebuke to correction

---

[8] See esp. Jer. 20:9.

and how his words draw from earlier Scriptures. We have also noticed how some twenty-nine times in this short book phrases such as *the word of the* LORD, *the voice of the* LORD and *declares the* LORD occur. This means that the content of what Haggai says is the word of God as well as the words of Haggai. As with the mystery of the givenness of the word so there is a mystery about how that becomes flesh in a human being.

The comparison of Haggai with his contemporary Zechariah is fascinating. Both spoke essentially the same message and both helped the returned exiles to take up the task again.[9] Yet neither could be mistaken for the other and each used words in a way that was char-acteristic of them. We have already seen that the differences should not be exaggerated, especially when we consider the eschatological material in Haggai 2, but there is some truth in seeing Haggai as the energizer of the work and Zechariah as the visionary who reveals the wider implications of that work.

Looking at Haggai's style we can discern a directness and a willing-ness to confront what is wrong which is the mark of the true prophet.[10] He shows an ability to anticipate the hearers' arguments, as in 1:5–11.[11] He speaks words which are new words for the present situation but which carry the weight also of earlier words spoken by earlier prophets.

We also see here a welcoming of the word of God. This has two sides. Leaders and people were genuinely moved by Haggai's words and their response was swift and their hearts were moved. The other side was that the Lord was moving in their hearts by his Spirit. These are two sides of the same coin. Without the Spirit no-one can respond to the word of God but it is all too possible to resist the Spirit and to be hardened against that word. Indeed that was the situation Malachi was to encounter.

b. God with us

At a time of great danger Isaiah had assured the people of God's presence.[12] Now at a very different time, Haggai reminds the people that this is not a mantra to be repeated but a reality to be realized. Central to this is the rebuilding of the temple and the reality of God's presence which it symbolized. Here the burden of Haggai's message

[9] Ezra 5:1–2.
[10] Other examples are: 'you are the man' (Nathan to David, 2 Sam. 12:7); 'I have not made trouble for Israel, but you and your father's family have' (Elijah to Ahab, 1 Kgs 18:18).
[11] Malachi does the same.
[12] Isa. 8:10.

is central to the whole flow of Scripture. God's purpose to be at the centre of his people and live with them will only fully be realized on the last day,[13] but the temple was a vital witness to that reality.

The presence of God is inseparable from the hearing of the word of God. If the temple is to be more than a building it must be the product of hearts and lives transformed by the word. Because God was not at the centre their economic as well as their spiritual lives were damaged. The fatal attraction of polytheism is that life can be divided into many segments and no 'god' claims absolute loyalty. To worship the Lord who made heaven and earth means a total commitment.

To speak of 'God with us' without true response of heart and life leads to two kinds of dangers. One is of a vague mysticism which imagines that repeating the words and having 'blessed thoughts' is what the phrase means. The prophets are always alive to this danger and Amos savagely castigates 'religion' which is in words and feelings but has no impact on lives.[14] Here in Haggai's day, the people are sunk in lethargy and faith has become an optional extra.

The other danger is legalism, where punctilious obedience to the letter of the law becomes more important than justice and love. Haggai is very aware of this problem, which is why he concentrates on covenant issues in his echoing of the covenant curses. This emphasis is underlined in verse 11 where God is described as *the LORD their God* and the relationship with him is to be the driving force of the renewed work. This idea will be developed eschatologically in chapter 2.

c. The divine and human elements

Just as the prophecy itself is both the word of the Lord and the words of Haggai, so the whole flow of the text and the development of the action is a blend of divine and human elements. The use of the words *stirred up* links this with the initial edict of Cyrus (Ezra 1:1). The dating of the prophecy in the *second year of King Darius* underlines the use of that king to continue God's purposes.[15] The theology here is that expressed in Daniel 4:35: 'He does as he pleases with the powers of heaven and the peoples of the earth. No-one can hold back his hand or say to him "What have you done?".' In chapter 2 this divine control of history is seen to extend to the very end of history and beyond.[16]

[13] Rev. 21:3.
[14] E.g. Amos 5:14–15.
[15] See Ezra 5 – 6.
[16] See also the exposition of Ezra 1.

A major part of that divine intervention is the prophetic word, which not only announces but moves those to whom it is announced. Haggai and Zechariah are described as helping the work of rebuilding.[17] Whatever else they did, it was their words which then inspired the work and which continue to speak to us millennia later. The living word is not limited by time or space, and what is true of the words of Haggai is true of the Bible as a whole.

The human element lies in the response. First, there is the response of the prophet. The messenger needs above all else to be faithful and say neither more nor less than what is given. The words spoken by Haggai and Zechariah were the first essential part of the human response – 'How shall they hear without someone preaching to them?' (Rom. 10:14). That word also met with a response in the hearts of leaders and people. Also, unknown to him, Darius was following the divine will in the policies he pursued.[18]

This short chapter is in the mainstream of revelation and deals with huge issues. The faithfulness of the Lord to his covenant promises, the sanctuary as continuing evidence of his grace and the continued sending of prophets, are all examples of the themes introduced. The next chapter is to take all these to a deeper level and give glimpses of the coming glory beyond the dreary present.

[17] Ezra 5:2.
[18] See Ezra 5 – 6.

Haggai 2:1–9
4. Better days are coming!

In chapter 2 the theme of temple building continues but it moves up a gear. We are, in C. S. Lewis' words, 'further up and further in'.[1] The emphasis here is on how this will vastly exceed anything in the past. Three short messages from the prophet bring encouragement, warning and expectancy for the future. We will take each of these in turn and also use them as part of a coherent whole. This is particularly important in relation to verses 10–19, which some see as out of place, but the exposition will show how the whole argument of the book is coherent and cumulative. Five matters will be considered as we look at the first message in 2:1–9.

1. The time of the prophecy

Nearly a month had passed since work had begun on the temple and probably there was little to show for it except clutter and mess. Baldwin points out that, apart from the sheer hard graft of repair without modern machinery, the *seventh month* was the time of major festivals when no work was allowed.[2] There would be a sense of the enormity of the task, and thus what was needed above all was a message of encouragement.

Before looking at the actual words of Haggai, the very timing itself has its own significant message. The *twenty-first day* was the last full day of the Feast of Tabernacles or Booths.[3] This festival celebrated the exodus from Egypt and this was symbolized by living in booths 'so that your descendants will know that I had the Israelites live in booths when I brought them out of Egypt' (Lev. 23:43). In the context of Haggai this is especially significant. Far from living in

---

[1] C. S. Lewis, *The Last Battle*, ch. 15.
[2] Baldwin, p. 46.
[3] See Lev. 23:33–43.

booths the people had been enjoying luxury in *panelled houses* (1:3), and thus the prophet's message would have been reinforced by the symbolism of the festival. Moreover, the other biblical uses of the word are relevant. In Job 27:18 it is used as a symbol of frailty and vulnerability, and a similar idea is found in Jonah 4:5. But it is also used in Isaiah 4:6 with the idea of protection where it speaks of the Lord as a shelter on the last day. These twin ideas of the weakness of the people and the power of the Lord are at the heart of Haggai's message of encouragement.

One further point about timing is that Solomon's temple was dedicated in the seventh month.[4] This was certainly continuity, and underlined the fact that what they were doing was rebuilding the old temple not constructing a new one. Yet the memory would probably be more depressing than encouraging and to that we now turn.

2. The contrast of past and present

Verse 3 speaks the thought that was in the peoples' hearts: The past was so much better; we can never achieve anything like that. Such a feeling is common today as we contemplate the apparently inexorable decline of the church in the Western world, not to say our own weaknesses and failures, and the danger is to look to some 'golden age' in the past. Probably the people lamented their lack of resources, both human and material, compared to those of Solomon. Undoubtedly nostalgia would colour the memories of the elderly people who had seen the first temple, but nostalgia is very seductive and would simply make the present situation seem even worse. Yet the prophet is shrewd as he forces them to face up to what they are actually feeling and admit their grievous disappointment, before he can give the message of encouragement with maximum effect.

There is, however, a clear difference between the peoples' discouragement here and their attitude at the beginning of chapter 1. There it had been apathy and complacency, which needed to be disturbed by words of challenge and rebuke. Here it was crippling despondency, which needed to be met by words of encouragement, and this is what comes next in the flow of the passage.

3. The word of encouragement

Verses 4 and 5 are a fine anatomy of how true encouragement comes. The first thing to notice is that this is spiritual rather than psychological. *Be strong*, says Haggai, *and work*. But the important point

[4] 1 Kgs 8:2.

is the reason he gives, not 'work because that gets things done' or 'work because you'll feel better if you do'. No – *work. For I am with you, declares the* LORD *Almighty.* The reality of the Lord's active and living presence is what will get the work done. Haggai does not deny the reality of the present situation – the mounds of rubble, the contrast with the past and the daunting task ahead. Rather he places these facts in the context of a greater reality. His method is like that of Elisha trapped with his servant in Dothan when the Syrian army with its forces and chariots surrounded the city.[5] Elisha does not deny that they are there but sees the greater reality of the horses and chariots of fire. His words to this terrified servant are, 'Those who are with us are more than those who are with them' (2 Kgs 6:16). That is, in effect, what Haggai is saying here.

The words *I am with you* were spoken to that earlier Joshua when the Lord pledged to him the same constant presence and protection experienced by Moses himself.[6] Indeed Moses had promised that to the whole nation in his closing words.[7] Similarly, Jacob, on his deathbed, says to Joseph 'I am about to die, but God will be with you' (Gen. 48:21). This is a promise which our Lord himself re-inforces in Matthew 28:20 where his presence and power is promised until the end of the age.

It is always a temptation in times of discouragement to long for the return of some great figure of the past; more often that reveals more of our preferences than a genuine spiritual insight. Haggai is saying, 'You are not going to have Moses, David or Solomon returning, but the living God is with you. He is working now as he worked in the past and, having begun a good work, he is going to complete it.'

So from a wrong view of the past where nostalgia leads to despair about the present, Haggai leads them to a true view of the past and of the unchanging faithfulness of the Lord. The covenant when they came out of Egypt was not simply another event in their history, it was the decisive revelation of their God and an assurance that he would be with them for ever. This is reinforced by the phrase *and my Spirit remains among you* (v. 5). This is also the conviction of Zechariah: 'Not by might nor by power, but by my Spirit' (4:6).

It is worth reflecting on the relationship between the Spirit's work and human work. Just as Haggai shows that human work without the Spirit will be futile, so he shows that human endeavour is an integral part of the Spirit's working. The fact that the Spirit is working is shown by the fact that his people are working. This does not mean

[5] 2 Kgs 6:8–17.
[6] Josh. 1:5.
[7] Deut. 31:6–7.

that God is dependent on any particular group of people, but it does mean that when the Spirit is at work, his word inspires people to do their tasks which may have previously seemed hopeless.

Moreover this is the same Spirit who gave Bezabel the gifts to construct the tabernacle.[8] In Numbers 11:17 the elders are given 'of the Spirit' that was in Moses. Isaiah 63:10–14 underlines the centrality of the Spirit in the exodus, both in the crossing of the sea and the journey through the desert. The Spirit, while manifesting himself particularly in the exodus, is not absent nor impotent at other times. We need to remember this in our day when we are often tempted to discount the Spirit's presence in the absence of the spectacular.[9] Fundamentally this is a call to see the ongoing work from the divine rather than the human perspective and to place it in the present in the context of God's ongoing work. Haggai has already shown the continuity of the present situation with the exodus and now he is about to look to the future and the ultimate realization of God's purposes.

4. The future universal significance of the house

The human effort now in place, Haggai develops the theme that the final splendour of the temple will be the result of God's direct actions. We move from the local to the universal and from the present to the future. This is very closely linked with the previous section with its emphasis on the exodus and similar divine help in the present.[10] This is the guarantee of future blessings. The continuity with the exodus is emphasized by the phrase *once more* (v. 6), which suggests that similar acts of God will happen.

Once again problems have been raised with the phrase *in a little while* (lit. 'it is a little'). However, the expression is important in underlining that Haggai is thinking of God's timetable rather than ours. Peter, echoing Psalm 90:4, points to the fact that with the Lord 'a thousand years are like a day' (2 Pet. 3:8). The emphasis on imminence has two implications. The first is that every generation must live in watchful expectancy: 'Therefore, keep watch, because

---

[8] Exod. 31:2–3; 35:30–31.

[9] Some have argued that v. 5a is an interpolation because the words do not occur in the LXX or the Peshitta. Also *kārat* ('to cut') is normally used with *běrît* ('covenant') rather than *hadābbār* ('the word'). Further it is alleged that it separates *I am with you* and *my Spirit remains with you*. None of these is convincing, especially since the omitted phrase is crucial for the exodus references in the text. Public speakers often insert extra phrases which further illuminate what they are saying. See further Motyer's demonstration of the structure of the verses (Motyer, 'Haggai').

[10] It is a pity that NIV in its characteristic desire for smooth flow omits the connective *kî*, 'for', which makes the link explicit.

you do not know the day or the hour' (Matt. 25:13). The other is that the event is certain; it is not simply that the coming of the kingdom is tagged on at the end, rather that God has been working to this end throughout history.

The language of God shaking *the heavens and the earth, the sea and the dry land*, is of theophany and occurs, for example, in Nahum 1:5, 'The mountains quake before him'. Here the whole of the physical creation trembles at his presence. Similar words are used of the exodus in Psalm 77:18 and of David's experience in Psalm 18:7. Ultimately the language points to the new heaven and the new earth. In one sense the whole Bible is an outworking of Genesis 1:1; the good creation, spoiled by sin, will be renewed and God's purposes from all eternity will be fulfilled. The whole created order will reflect the beauty of the Creator and the curse of Genesis 3 will be removed. The Hebrew word *shake* here is a participle, which suggests a number of shakings and a number of interventions in history before the final shaking which ushers in the kingdom.

The shaking will affect the nations as well as the physical universe and will result in their bringing their treasures to the temple (v. 7). This can be understood on a number of levels, all related to God's kingship over the nations and his ownership of the silver and gold. At the most basic level this was happening as Darius instructed the opponents of the temple building to pay the cost of the project from the royal revenue in their own taxation districts.[11] It was further fulfilled when Herod undertook extensive works to beautify the structure.[12] These were partial fulfilments but by no means do they exhaust the meaning, for neither heralded a movement among the nations to bring their treasures to the Lord's house.

Discussion of this passage has been complicated by traditional messianic interpretation. The most striking proponent of this view is probably E. B. Pusey[13] who based this comment on the KJV translation: 'the desire of all nations shall come, and I will fill this house with glory.' He argues that this must refer to Christ whom the nations longed for, often subconsciously. Grammatically, Pusey is on shaky ground because *ḥemdat* is singular but the verb is plural.[14]

[11] See above on Ezra 6:8–10.
[12] Reflected in the comments of Mark 13:1.
[13] See his *Minor Prophets, vol. VII, Zephaniah and Haggai* (London: Nisbet, 1907), pp. 247–255.
[14] R. W. L. Moberley subjects Pusey's interpretation to a merciless critique and demonstrates that he has ignored grammar in pursuit of a particular interpretation. That is fair enough, but as I have tried to demonstrate, the eschatological interpretation is sound and does not need strained exegesis to establish it. See, 'How May We Speak to God? A Reconsideration of the Nature of Biblical Theology', *Tyndale Bulletin* 53:2 (2002), pp. 179–184.

However, if the interpretation given here is correct, the eschatological meaning is the only one which does justice to the verse even if the Messiah is not explicitly mentioned. This richness of allusion is something we have noticed already in Haggai and, for that matter, in Ezra.

But more fundamental is the fulfilment of the passage both at Christ's first and second comings. Malachi also spoke more specifically of this: 'Suddenly the Lord you are seeking will come to this temple' (Mal. 3:1). Jesus' death caused the curtain of the temple to be torn from top to bottom, accompanied by a shaking of the earth;[15] a greater shaking marked the resurrection.[16] But the final fulfilment lies in the future when 'the Lord God and the Lamb' *are* the temple (Rev. 21:22).

We need to hold all these ideas together if we are to do justice to what Haggai saying here. The spiritual interpretation of verse 8 does not contradict the material interpretation, rather they are both needed to show that the fulfilment is neither limited to physical resources nor an idealistic dream.

These ideas are reinforced by verse 9. *This present house* refers to the entire history of the temple through all its changes and chances. *Glory* is the visible presence of God himself which both fills the whole earth[17] and is manifested partially in the temple but fully in Jesus Christ.[18] The additional idea is that the temple will be a place of *peace*. The immediate contrast is that the temple fell in savage war and bloodshed; its rebuilding was hindered by opposition but now it is to proceed to completion. Yet once again that far from exhausts its meaning.

'Peace', as Baldwin says, 'sums up all the blessings of the Messianic age, when reconciliation with God and His righteous rule will ensure a just and lasting peace'.[19] Peace is first a restored relationship with God and then a stable and happy society and redeemed and satisfied individuals. Here it is a gift of God himself who will, by the death and resurrection of Christ bring the true blessings of peace to all who receive them.

The broader interpretation of these verses is confirmed by their use in Hebrews 12:26–27. The result of God's shakings of the physical universe will be a kingdom which cannot be shaken. This is the climax of a passage which speaks of Mount Zion the heavenly Jerusalem and the festival gathering where the reality of the worship

---

[15] Matt. 27:51.
[16] Matt. 28:2.
[17] Isa. 6:3.
[18] John 1:14.
[19] Baldwin, p. 49.

of God is experienced in a way that brings together and supersedes all earlier glimpses of the presence.

5. General comments

This is a rich passage and shows the power of the prophet's vision as he outlines the prospects for the coming age. Two particular matters are worth reflecting on as we survey these verses.

a. Blend of divine and human activity

The sense of God at work is palpable and electrifying. It is instructive to study the number of verbs with the Lord as subject, especially in verses 6–9: *I will shake, I will fill, I will grant*. The establishing of the kingdom and its accompanying blessings will be wholly a divine activity which will be accomplished irrespective of human strength or weakness. This must always be the ground of our security and our impetus for persevering.

Yet the actual building was part of the whole movement of the story. It might seem a far cry from this building site to the heavenly city, but this part of the story was a necessary part of the big story. It is not so much that God had his part to play and humans did as well. Rather the work of God's Spirit is evident in the changed hearts of the people which led them to resume the work and to bring it to the completion we read of in Ezra 6:15–22. Vital in this was the words of the prophet as the link between God's grace and human defeat.

b. Progressive fulfilment of prophecy

Peter tells us that the prophets were 'men who spoke from God as they were carried along by the Holy Spirit' (2 Pet. 1:21). This is a specific illustration of the above point about divine and human activity. The human authorship is real – 'men spoke', but the authorship is 'from God', and it is the work of the Spirit which produces the message. This means that the words of Haggai speak directly to the situation of 520 BC and the aborted temple building project, and that is where our interpretation of what he says must begin. Yet to confine the message to them and to the further building activities of Herod is to miss the abiding relevance and eternal significance of the prophet's words.

Eschatological fulfilment is the ultimate significance of the prophecy. In Haggai's own day that did not produce unrealistic visionaries but rather those who laboured faithfully in their own day. Heeding his words will have the same effect in our or any other day.

Haggai 2:10–19
5. Count your blessings

Nearly four months have passed since Haggai's initial message in 1:1–2, and two months since the glowing words of 2:1–9. God's voice has not been silent, however, for Zechariah had begun his ministry a month previously.[1] The final section, like the previous one, is to concentrate on a vision of the future, but the current one appears to be a digression and discrepancies have been found between this passage and Ezra 3:10–13.[2] Also attempts have been made to remove 2:15–19 and place it after 1:15a (we shall discuss that further in the exposition). The initial point though is that this chapter, indeed the whole book, is a unity with clear development of thought with both a chronological and theological rationale. What we must do is to ask how this section flows from 2:1–9 and anticipates 2:20–23.

1. Reasons for the message

Three reasons for its position in the chapter can be suggested.

a) Theological

Psalm 93:5 says 'Holiness adorns your house for endless days, O LORD'. This has implications not only for the heavenly city where 'nothing impure will ever enter' (Rev. 21:27), but for the temple building and the lives of the temple builders there and then. The

---

[1] Zech. 1:1.
[2] J. W. Rothstein in *Juden and Samaritaner: Die grundlegende Scheidung von Judentum and Heidentum* (Leipzig, 1908) argued that 'the day when the foundation of the Lord's temple was laid' (v. 18) refers to another foundation in 520 BC rather than in 536 BC. He further argues that 'this people' (v. 14) are the Samaritan opponents of the building. But the phrase has already been used in 1:2 and it would be odd to use it with a different meaning here. See further the exposition.

essence of the new heaven and earth is a restored and vital relationship with the Lord, and the role of the temple on earth, whether the old temple or the new temple of living stones, is to anticipate that. Holiness was not to be confined to the temple precincts. The idea that there is a special place where 'religious' activities occur and a 'secular' space where God is not important is to be rejected. When this happens neither the so-called 'saved' or the so-called 'secular' prosper because the basic integrity of response to God in the whole of life is lacking. If this community and its temple are to be truly an anticipation of the world to come they must be holy.

b) Pragmatic

This flows from the theological necessity of holiness. The prophecy of the shaking of heaven and earth and the coming glory of the house is necessary to give courage and perseverance in the present. However, it is just there that another temptation arises, and that is to neglect the present demands or indeed see them as of little relevance. This is a problem which Paul also had to deal with.[3] The people needed to be recalled to the realities of the situation: the as yet uncompleted temple, the economic downturn and the relevance to these of basic demands of the Torah. This is the emphasis of verse 18–19, which underline the message of 1:1–11 with the repetition of the phrase *give careful thought* or 'consider'.

c) Eschatological

Verse 19 ends *from this day on I will bless you*. 'Bless' could easily be taken as material and refer to economic prosperity, and indeed that is part of the meaning. Malachi 3:8–11 shows that some fifty years later poor economic conditions were prevalent, and once again the prophet links that with failure in giving to the Lord with glad hearts. But, as we will see in the next section (2:20–23) the full meaning of his word is eschatological.

So, very far from these verses being misplaced, they form an effective bridge between a prophecy of ultimate blessing and the further prophecy to Zerubbabel, and they link the present and the eternal. Once again the oracle is introduced with a precise time note which in our calendar would be 18 December. By that time the autumn rains would have fallen and the winter crops sown, reminding the people of their entire dependence on the Creator. Five matters call for consideration.

---

[3] See 2 Thess. 3:6–13.

2. The duty of the priests to teach

Verse 12 shows this clearly, *Ask the priests what the law says*. Priests were never intended to be simply liturgical functionaries; they were also expected to teach Torah. Malachi is to castigate them for failing in both these functions.[4] Leviticus 10:11 speaks of the task of Aaron and his sons to 'teach the Israelites all the decrees that the LORD has given them through Moses'. This is developed in Deuteronomy 17:9–12 where not only do the priests have the task of teaching the revelation but also of making decisions about difficult cases not specifically covered in the Torah. Indeed it could be argued that the prophets were raised up when the priests failed to fulfil their ministry; without teaching of the word of God the church will be anaemic and ineffective. Presumably Haggai and Zechariah were given their messages from the Lord because the priests who had returned from Babylon failed to teach the people.

3. Holiness is not contagious but unholiness is

Haggai never uses question and answer (as Malachi does) to show the art of the teacher. Presumably, *consecrated meat* would be from one of the offerings such as the sin offering, part of which was given to the priests and thus frequently carried in their robes.[5] Holiness is not communicated from it to anything else. However, defilement is passed on by contact, which is Haggai's main point here. The law says that anything touched by an unclean person becomes unclean itself.[6]

The point of this is the application in verse 14: people who are unholy do not become holy simply by engaging in religious activities. To work in 'saved space' does not make the work holy if hearts and motives are wrong. But Haggai is also echoing 1:5–6 where economic and social life had gone sour because of the fact that the people were not right with God. *Whatever they do and whatever they offer* is a comprehensive summing up of the whole of their lives. At the heart of the Torah stood the words of the Lord: 'Be holy because I, the LORD your God, am holy' (Lev. 19:2). That chapter in Leviticus is a neat summary of both the worship requirements and lifestyle obligations of God's people. When Peter takes up these words in his first letter he similarly blends the theological and practical.[7] Thus what we have here is not a trifling regulation about consecrated meat but

[4] See esp. Mal. 2:1–9.
[5] Lev. 6:25–29.
[6] Num. 19:22.
[7] 1 Pet. 1:15–16.

a profound observation on the holiness of God and its implications for his people's lives. Baldwin[8] perceptively points out that the ruined temple was like a corpse in the midst, which gave the lie to Israel being a holy nation.[9] This was not then and is not now an easy message to hear. We tend to like hearing of enjoyment and fulfilling our potential. Neither of these are wrong in themselves; indeed they are gifts of God. But before we can enjoy the blessing of verse 19 we need to put our house in order and strive for holiness.

4. The need for discernment

To understand truly the times in which they were living more than a nasty look was needed. *Give careful thought*, says Haggai, and *consider how things were*. He is now moving from an unfolding of the situation to a necessary response to it. Once again the everyday circumstances and amenities of living are a window to the larger purposes of God and the big picture; for what the prophet says here is that these are a direct consequence of the fact that God is Creator and has revealed himself in his word. The truth of the unity of life both 'sacred' and 'secular' had been underlined in verse 14, now here it is spelled out. The building of the temple was related ultimately to the way the Creator had made the universe, and the failure of their material prosperity and the weather conditions were the external signs of the failure of the devotion of their hearts to the Lord. Any possibility of this being coincidental is ruled out by verse 17: *I struck all the work of your hands with blight, mildew and hail.* These events were already a message to those who had read the Torah where such calamities were predicted for failure to obey the covenant.[10] But it needed a prophet to show to that generation, just as Amos had done to an earlier one,[11] that God's words were living and always brought about what they said whether in judgment or blessing.

We should not ignore the phrase *from this day on* (v. 18), repeated in verse 19. God's word is no vague and disembodied entity; it comes at precise moments, which can often be specifically dated, and this is common in the prophets, especially in Isaiah, Jeremiah and Ezekiel. A definite and considered response is needed to this word of God or its effect will be lost. Again the failure of the harvest is linked with the failure to continue with the rebuilding of the temple. None of this is obvious on the surface of events; careful thought and determination to act on the prophetic word is vital.

[8] Baldwin, p. 51.
[9] Exod. 19:6.
[10] See esp. Deut. 28:22.
[11] Amos 4:9.

Truly to believe in the biblical doctrine of God as Creator is far more than simply acknowledging the existence of the first cause. That is deism and has no effect on our thinking and living. But the biblical doctrine is of a Creator who is intimately involved in this creation and to whom we owe everything we are and have and who is not far from each one of us.[12] This has a radical effect on thinking and living and sees the whole of life as of concern and interest to the Lord. Indeed this essential unity and integrity of life is presupposed in the Shema: 'Hear, O Israel: the LORD our God, the LORD is one' (Deut. 6:4). This means that the whole of life belongs to the Lord, unlike paganism where allegiance is divided among many gods who can then be played off against each other. This divided heart lies at the root of so much of the staleness and fruitlessness of much church activity. To fail to see that the world of worship and work belong to and flow from the same God is to opt for a life where what we profess and how we live become increasingly divorced. This attitude, which in theory believes in the Lord, but wants to keep him away from the 'real' concerns of living, always creates a low spiritual temperature and a complacent and apathetic mindset.

5. The reality of God's blessing

From this day on I will bless you (v. 19). Just as blight, mildew and hail were a sign of the curse which followed from disobedience[13] so now God was to bestow covenant blessing. Blessing is no mere formality; the Creator is pledging that there will be new life, for this word carries rich associations of creation and covenant and of a future bright beyond our imagination. God blesses Adam and Eve[14] and this blessing carries the promise of fruitfulness, a promise repeated to Noah in Genesis 9:1 and repeated again in fourfold promise to Abraham.[15] This situation, low-key and uninspiring as it appeared, was a new and significant part of the great story leading to the new creation. Beyond and above human failure and sin is the overarching grace of God.

Blessing here means that God's ancient purposes in creation and salvation will be fulfilled. The harvest and the temple are linked again but this time positively. The Lord's purpose will be fulfilled and his people need to be obedient. Malachi speaks in similar terms of bringing 'the whole tithe into the storehouse' (Mal. 3:10), which will be followed by blessings raining down from heaven. This was so

[12] Acts 17:27.
[13] Deut. 28:22.
[14] Gen. 1:28.
[15] Gen 12:2–3.

much more than hoping for a good harvest; it was a commitment of the covenant Lord and as such is a promise for all of life and beyond.

6. God accommodates himself to our weaknesses

This is well expressed by Calvin,[16] who recognizes that the deprivation of earthly blessings is sometimes the way in which God teaches his people to lay up treasure in heaven. But here the prophet wants to teach the people that their own labour was irrelevant if God did not bless, and not to state as an invariable rule that God blesses every activity we undertake. A number of considerations flow from this.

The first is that God, while utterly consistent, speaks in a variety of ways related to the spiritual maturity of the hearers. The exile had burned much of the idolatry out of them, but they were still far from a living and joyful faith. They were apathetic and needed the incentive of future blessing to rouse them from their torpor and their spiritual sluggishness. This is an important principle for those who bring God's word to people. That word does not vary, but the way in which it is presented and its particular emphases will be adapted to the capacity of the hearers. Here, the problem Haggai identified at the beginning (1:4) is that a love of earthly possession and security had gripped the returned exiles. Haggai realizes that the first step must be to show them that there was no security in *panelled houses* and that instead of being shrewd they were in fact behaving foolishly. Calvin says:

> As men, for the most part, on account of their ignorance, cannot be led at first to this generous state of mind, so as to devote themselves willingly to God, it is necessary to begin by using other means, as the Prophet does here, who promises earthly and daily sustenance to the Jews, for he saw that they could not immediately, at the first step, ascend upwards to heaven.[17]

Second, while God is constantly gracious with our failings, he leaves us in no doubt that he is the author of everything good. This is confirmed by the use of the word *bless*. Here is not a gospel of good works. Rather God is saying through the prophet that these material blessings are an anticipation of yet greater blessings to come (which are to be outlined in the final section of the book).

The third consideration is that the promise of blessing is also a call to radical faith, more than ever needed in a situation where the

---

[16] Calvin, pp. 382–383; the two paragraphs repay close study.
[17] Calvin, p. 383.

outward signs of God's presence seemed insignificant. This was the middle of the growing season, and faith and obedience were needed to see that taking time away from work in the fields to work on the temple would in fact mean a better harvest. This promise opens the door for new beginnings and a change of heart that is in itself an evidence of blessing.

We can see the importance now of this section sandwiched between two pictures of the future. The emphasis on holiness is both a powerful reminder of the Torah and a pointer to the holiness which will be at the heart of the new creation.[18] The whole of life is a unity, and if the temple on earth is to reflect the temple in heaven there must be no separate secular[19] and religious aspects of life. It further shows the centrality of our thought life (vv. 15, 18) and the continual need to assess what we are doing in the light of the word of God.

---

[18] Rev. 21:27.

[19] 'Secular' is, of course, an anachronism, but it points to the kind of behaviour which is essentially pagan in that it denies God's lordship over the whole of life.

Haggai 2:20–23
6. The best is yet to be

With this final oracle Haggai ends on a high note and while summing up some things already said goes far beyond these and points to a glorious future. The word *bless* (v. 19) is now given both a specific and an eternal emphasis which underline the importance of the present situation and places it in the wider sweep of God's purposes. Four matters call for comment.

1. There will be universal upheaval

From the human perspective this is the rubble and clutter of a building site; from God's perspective this is a vital link in the chain which leads through all the convulsions of history such as flood, Sodom, exile and the like to the great convulsion that will herald the coming of the new creation.[1] As mentioned in the exposition of verses 6 and 7, this shaking is already seen in the first coming of Christ but remains to be fully realized when he comes again.[2]

It is always vital that those working for God, especially in times of little visible growth, should see what they are doing in the widest perspective. The rebuilding of the temple seemed a world away from the glorious vision of the mountain of the Lord to which the nations would come and yet it was part of the process that would lead to that day. This is the reason, probably, why the promise is given twice. However, this prediction of universal upheaval is not simply a repetition of verses 6 and 7, and that leads us to the second main concern of this section.

---

[1] 2 Pet. 3:10.
[2] Thus I think Calvin is wrong, when he fails to see in these other events the fore-shadowing of the kingdom. Calvin, p. 385.

2. All other powers will be overthrown

In verses 6–9 the emphasis had been on glory and splendour; here it is on the removal of all rival kingdoms. As the prophets look into the future, guided by the Holy Spirit, what is revealed to them is consistent with the particular circumstances in which they minister. The exiles had indeed returned, but the tiny province in which they were was insignificant in the eyes of the world, and was not an independent kingdom. It had no military muscle and there seemed no prospect of the Davidic kingdom occupying the position it once did. Here is the answer: the Lord who brought his people out of Egypt and raised up the Davidic dynasty will do this. The words are less poetic but point to the same reality as Isaiah 9:2–7.

Two emphases stand out. The first is that God will destroy the rival seats[3] of power and remove all opposition at its source. The *power of the foreign kingdoms* will be destroyed (again the picture in Dan. 2 of the stone striking the kingdoms of the world is a parallel). The other is that God will remove the specific manifestations of these powers, symbolized here by horses, chariots and riders (perhaps an allusion to Exod. 15:1, 4, 19, 21). The reference to the armies destroying each other recalls Ezekiel 38:21 where God and Magog turn against each other, and Zechariah's vision of a similar conflict in the winding up of history.[4] Evil is destroyed by God but it also is inherently self destructive.

This remains an important message for us when we are overwhelmed at the global power of nations, multi-national enterprises and the ever-growing influence of huge media corporations. It is easy to be intimidated by the progressive secularization of life in the West, the rapid dismantling of our Christian heritage and the relentless sneering of the media at biblical Christianity. But we do not need to tremble for the ark of God as Eli did,[5] for Christ is building his church and nothing can prevent that. This is no mere abstract idea and Haggai now makes this specific for his own day as well as anticipating what is yet to come.

3. The messianic significance of Zerubbabel

We have already seen that our knowledge of Zerubbabel is slight and we do not know what happened to him (he is not mentioned in the account of the temple's completion in Ezra 6:15). In one sense, like

---

[3] *Royal thrones* is in fact singular; this probably refers to the symbol of kingship and ultimately the godless power (as in Dan. 7) which is behind human regimes.
[4] Zech. 14:13.
[5] 1 Sam. 4:13.

the rebuilt temple itself, he seems a minor player. But as we have already seen in relation to the temple, so in relation to Zerubbabel, to look on that event and this individual as insignificant is to miss the point.

In 1:1, 14; 2:2, 21 Zerubbabel is simply called *governor*, but here in verse 23 he is *my servant*. Not only is that a regular term for Moses and David,[6] but it is used extensively by Isaiah;[7] thus Zerubbabel is a vital link in the chain leading to the true Messiah in whom the functions of priest and king would perfectly combine. Some have argued that Zechariah 4:6–10 sees Zerubbabel's role simply as temple builder rather than great military leader.[8] That is to miss the point. Haggai makes it plain that it is not Zerubbabel but the Lord who will win the battle and that it is the Messiah who will inherit the kingdom. Moreover, Zechariah's emphasis is on the power of the Spirit to flatten mountains, and although to the observer it may seem a 'day of small things' (Zech. 4:10), yet God is powerfully at work. Thus the work of the kingdom is always of eternal significance whatever may be the outward circumstances. Most strikingly, Zerubbabel appears in the genealogy of Jesus in Matthew 1:13, which underlines his vital significance.

Seeing Zerubbabel as a messianic figure is another indication of how God is preparing his people through the centuries for what he is to do fully and finally in Christ. Motyer writes 'God had acted "typically" and characteristically in certain great persons and events of the past, and, because God does not change, he will so act again'.[9] The prominence of David points, however partially, to the victories and glory of the one to come; a more obscure figure such as Zerubbabel points to the humility and hiddenness. Only when the kingdom finally comes will all varying emphases and paradoxes be resolved. *On that day*[10] (v. 23) is a prophetic shorthand for the day of the Lord and thus impels us to the future and to the day when God will be God and the world will know it. All this is guaranteed by the word of the Lord, and this brings us to the fourth strand in this section.

---

[6] E.g. Josh. 1:2; 2 Kgs 19:34.

[7] See Isa. 41:8; 42:1; 49:5–6; 50:10; 52:13; 53:11.

[8] E.g. Lex Mason in 'Zerubbabel', in W. VanGemeren (ed.), *New International Dictionary of Old Testament Theology and Exegesis*, vol. 4 (Carlisle: Paternoster Press, 1996), p. 1313.

[9] J. A. Motyer, 'Messiah: In the Old Testament', in J. W. Douglas (ed.), *Illustrated Bible Dictionary*, Part 2 (Leicester: IVP, 1980), p. 988.

[10] *On that day* or 'in those days' occurs throughout the prophets, e.g. Isa. 11:10; 19:23; Jer. 4:9; 48:41; Ezek. 29:21; Amos 9:13; Obad. 8; Mic. 5:10; Zech. 12:3; Mal. 4:1.

4. The signet ring is the token of God's favour

The signet ring was precious to the wearer, who would take care of it and cherish it. This idea is well expressed in Song of Songs 8:6: 'Place me like a seal over your heart, like a seal on your arm.' It was also a mark of authenticity and authority.[11] In Jeremiah 22:24 God removes the signet ring from Jehoiachin as a sign that the kingdom is doomed to exile. But here it is given to Zerubbabel to show that the messianic line continues.

This is a sign to the world that God has good purposes for Zerubbabel and that he represented in his day the promise to David in spite of the exile. It is worth reading and reflecting on Psalm 89 in this connection. That psalm speaks of 'David my servant' (v. 20) who will be 'the most exalted of the kings of the earth' (v. 27). That is not set aside by the punishment of the exile (v. 32), which is followed by an underlining of the covenant with David in verses 33–37: 'his line will continue for ever and his throne endure before me like the sun.' The tension remains in the psalm because until Christ came and comes again it needs faith and endurance. Kidner has a characteristically penetrating comment: 'Instead of railing at the promise or explaining it away, it faces the full clash of word and event in an appeal to God to show his hand. Like unresolved discord it therefore impels us towards the New Testament, where we find that the fulfilment will altogether outstrip the expectation.'[12]

This further linked with God's providence: *for I have chosen you* (v. 23). God made a covenant with David: 'I took you from the pasture and from following the flock to be ruler over my people Israel' (2 Sam. 7:8), and now that covenant is renewed with Zerubbabel. This is further reinforced by the last words of the book: *declares the LORD Almighty*. This is no wishful thinking, this is trusting in God who has committed himself to his people by promises that he cannot and will not break.

5. Conclusions on Haggai

Inevitably, as we come to the end of this little book questions remain, not least about the prophet himself. I am sure I am not the only person who has often wished that he had an authoritative supplement to the Bible giving us information about many of the individuals who appear briefly in its pages and then vanish (we have already

[11] Some examples would be Pharaoh giving his seal to Joseph (Gen. 41:42) and Ahasuerus sealing royal edicts (Esth. 3:10; 8:8–10).
[12] F. D. Kidner, *Psalms 73–150*, Tyndale OT Commentaries (London: IVP, 1975), p. 319.

made a similar comment on Zerubbabel himself). There are many prophets of whom we know nothing (e.g. Nahum, Habakkuk and Malachi) but here we are given precise dates for only a very short period of Haggai's life.

We have already noted in the introduction to the exposition that the fact he is called a *prophet* suggests he is well known, but whether that was as a result of the prophecies here or whether he was already known we cannot tell. Nor do we know whether these short months happened in his early or later years. We know that the teachers of God's word both in Old and New Testaments spoke many things not recorded in Scripture. What is unusual is for such a short period to have such a powerful effect.

Of course we cannot know the answer to these questions. What we do know is that God raised up this prophet at the critical time and gave him a message for that time, but also made certain that the message became part of Scripture and thus valid for all times. As we come to the end of our study of Haggai there are three observations that will help to sum up something of what we have discovered.

a) Haggai is concise but his language is rich and resonant

It is almost mandatory to contrast Haggai with Zechariah, who is seen as a visionary and a poet while Haggai is a plain, blunt man who delivers a practical and down-to-earth message. There is an element of truth in that: God does call and use different personalities and employs the gifts and talents he has given them. But it obscures the more important fact that both spoke the word of the Lord and therein lay their significance and authority.

What is true is that Haggai is brief compared to Zechariah but, as we have seen, that brevity is the kind of conciseness that is full of depth and riches. This arises from a number of factors. The first is his sense of earlier Scriptures and of continuity with that revelation already given. Another is ability to strike right to the heart of the matter and stir people by showing the wider significance of the work they are doing. The third is his repeated emphasis that these are the Lord's words, which shows that they go far beyond good advice or shrewd observation.

b) Haggai blends rebuke and encouragement

He begins with rebuke and exhortation to stir people out of apathy but soon comes to encouragement and promise. This blend is particularly effective in the circumstances of the time. Unlike, say, Amos or Jeremiah, he is not faced with blatant idolatry, rather with a lack of vision and a failure to realize the greatness of God. We may suppose that many who had returned were motivated less by a living faith in God than by hopes of recovering the good old days. When that failed to materialize they became lukewarm – the promised land between the Nile and the Euphrates had shrunk to a small area surrounding Jerusalem. Mere denunciation would simply have evoked deeper gloom and given no incentive to continue the work. Yet rebuke was also necessary to show that it was entirely God's grace that they had returned at all.

But this encouragement is not mere fine words. This is related to God's purposes. Ezekiel had said 'Then the nations will know that I the LORD make Israel holy, when my sanctuary is among them forever' (37:28). Hence the single-minded concentration of Haggai on the necessity for rebuilding the temple. Like all the post-exilic writers, Haggai insists on the continuity of the returned exiles with the past people of God. Thus the encouragement flows from that conviction, especially in the messianic status of Zerubbabel and the hope of future blessing, which leads us to the third observation.

c) Haggai has both a timely and a timeless message

Failure to realize this has often led to a devaluing of the book. Some see it as ritualistic, over-emphasizing bricks and mortar, and a dull reflection of a dull time. Others with more of an eye to contemporary relevance preach sermons from chapter 1 about giving to the building fund and fail entirely to mention the spiritual temple. The key to avoiding both errors is to see the book as a vital link in the developing Bible story which finds its centre in Christ.

Ezekiel had portrayed the departure of the glory of the Lord from the temple to the summit of the Mount of Olives. Even there we can sense among the pain and anguish a glimpse of better things to come if we fit it into the big picture. Ezekiel says that the glory of the Lord 'stopped above the mountain' (Ezek. 11:23). Flash forward to Luke 24:50, where again the glory of the Lord, this time in human form, stands on the mountain. This time, though, it is blessing rather than judgment, as the great High Priest, his work on earth done, lifts his hands before ascending into the heavenly temple. That illustrates why Haggai's message is so essential, standing between the destruction of the temple in Ezekiel's day and the work of the one greater than the temple. O. Palmer Robertson puts it well: 'The people of the exile had to return to the land and the temple had to be rebuilt in order to provide a sanctified theatre in which the great acts of divine redemption could be brought to completion.'[13]

The temple for Haggai is so much more than a building, even a sacred one. It is the visible sign of God dwelling among his people by his Spirit (2:4–5).

So this little book is an encouragement and challenge, especially in days when the cause of Christ seems in such decline in the West and the temptation to give up or fall away is abundant. For those who preach the book it is a divine commentary on how God's purposes are never thwarted, as well as a ringing call to faithfulness.

[13] P. 375.

The Bible Speaks Today: Old Testament series

The Message of Genesis 1 – 11
The dawn of creation
David Atkinson

The Message of Genesis 12 – 50
From Abraham to Joseph
Joyce G. Baldwin

The Message of Exodus
The days of our pilgrimage
Alec Motyer

The Message of Leviticus
Free to be holy
Derek Tidball

The Message of Numbers
Journey to the promised land
Raymond Brown

The Message of Deuteronomy
Not by bread alone
Raymond Brown

The Message of Judges
Grace abounding
Michael Wilcock

The Message of Ruth
The wings of refuge
David Atkinson

The Message of Samuel
Personalities, potential, politics and power
Mary Evans

The Message of Chronicles
One church, one faith, one Lord
Michael Wilcock

The Message of Ezra and Haggai
Building for God
Robert Fyall

The Message of Nehemiah
God's servant in a time of change
Raymond Brown

The Message of Esther
God present but unseen
David G. Firth

The Message of Job
Suffering and grace
David Atkinson

The Message of Psalms
1 – 72
Songs for the people of God
Michael Wilcock

The Message of Psalms
73 – 150
Songs for the people of God
Michael Wilcock

The Message of Proverbs
Wisdom for life
David Atkinson

The Message of Ecclesiastes
A time to mourn, and a time to dance
Derek Kidner

The Message of the Song of Songs
The lyrics of love
Tom Gledhill

The Message of Isaiah
On eagles' wings
Barry Webb

The Message of Jeremiah
Against wind and tide
Derek Kidner

The Bible Speaks Today: New Testament series

The Message of the Sermon on the Mount (Matthew 5 – 7)
Christian counter-culture
John Stott

The Message of Matthew
The kingdom of heaven
Michael Green

The Message of Mark
The mystery of faith
Donald English

The Message of Luke
The Saviour of the world
Michael Wilcock

The Message of John
Here is your King
Bruce Milne

The Message of Acts
To the ends of the earth
John Stott

The Message of Romans
God's good news for the world
John Stott

The Message of 1 Corinthians
Life in the local church
David Prior

The Message of 2 Corinthians
Power in weakness
Paul Barnett

The Message of Galatians
Only one way
John Stott

The Message of Ephesians
God's new society
John Stott

The Message of Philippians
Jesus our Joy
Alec Motyer

The Message of Colossians and Philemon
Fullness and freedom
Dick Lucas

The Message of Thessalonians
Preparing for the coming King
John Stott

The Message of 1 Timothy and Titus
The life of the local church
John Stott

The Message of 2 Timothy
Guard the gospel
John Stott

The Message of Hebrews
Christ above all
Raymond Brown

The Message of James
The tests of faith
Alec Motyer

The Message of 1 Peter
The way of the cross
Edmund Clowney

The Message of 2 Peter and Jude
The promise of his coming
Dick Lucas and Christopher Green

The Message of John's Letters
Living in the love of God
David Jackman

The Message of Revelation
I saw heaven opened
Michael Wilcock

The Bible Speaks Today: Bible Themes series

The Message of the Living God
His glory, his people, his world
Peter Lewis

The Message of the Resurrection
Christ is risen!
Paul Beasley-Murray

The Message of the Cross
Wisdom unsearchable, love indestructible
Derek Tidball

The Message of Salvation
By God's grace, for God's glory
Philip Graham Ryken

The Message of Creation
Encountering the Lord of the universe
David Wilkinson

The Message of Heaven and Hell
Grace and destiny
Bruce Milne

The Message of Mission
The glory of Christ in all time and space
Howard Peskett and
Vinoth Ramachandra

The Message of Prayer
Approaching the throne of grace
Tim Chester

The Message of the Trinity
Life in God
Brian Edgar

The Message of Evil and Suffering
Light into darkness
Peter Hicks

The Message of the Holy Spirit
The Spirit of encounter
Keith Warrington

The Message of Holiness
Restoring God's masterpiece
Derek Tidball